The WAC Journal

Writing Across the Curriculum
Volume 25
2014

© 2014 Clemson University
Printed on acid-free paper in the USA
ISSN: 1544-4929

Editor

Roy Andrews

Managing Editor

Heather Christiansen, Clemson University

Associate Editors

David Blakesley, Clemson University
Michael LeMahieu, Clemson University

Editorial Board

Art Young, Clemson University
Neal Lerner, Northeastern University
Carol Rutz, Carleton College
Meg Petersen, Plymouth State University
Terry Myers Zawacki, George Mason Univ.

Review Board

Jacob S. Blumner, Univ of Michigan, Flint
Patricia Donahue, Lafayette College
John Eliason, Gonzaga University
Michael LeMahieu, Clemson University
Neal Lerner, Northeastern University
Meg Petersen, Plymouth State University
Mya Poe, Northeastern University
Carol Rutz, Carleton College
Joanna Wolfe, University of Louisville
Terry Myers Zawacki, George Mason Univ.
David Zehr, Plymouth State University

Subscription Information

The WAC Journal
Parlor Press
3015 Brackenberry Drive
Anderson SC 29621
wacjournal@parlorpress.com
parlorpress.com/wacjournal
Rates: 1 year: $25; 3 years: $65; 5 years: $95.

Submissions

The editorial board of *The WAC Journal* seeks WAC-related articles from across the country. Our national review board welcomes inquiries, proposals, and 3,000 to 6,000 word articles on WAC-related topics, including the following: WAC Techniques and Applications; WAC Program Strategies; WAC and WID; WAC and Writing Centers; Interviews and Reviews. Proposals and articles outside these categories will also be considered. Any discipline-standard documentation style (MLA, APA, etc.) is acceptable, but please follow such guidelines carefully. Submissions are managed initially via Submittable (https://parlorpress.submittable.com/submit) and then via email. For general inquiries, contact Heather Christiansen, the managing editor, via email (wacjournal@parlorpress.com). The WAC Journal is an open-access, blind, peer-viewed journal published annually by Clemson University, Parlor Press, and the WAC Clearinghouse. It is available in print through Parlor Press and online in open-access format at the WAC Clearinghouse. *The WAC Journal* is peer-reviewed. It is published annually by Clemson University, Parlor Press, and the WAC Clearinghouse.

Subscriptions

The WAC Journal is published annually in print by Parlor Press and Clemson University. Digital copies of the journal are simultaneously published at The WAC Clearinghouse in PDF format for free download. Print subscriptions support the ongoing publication of the journal and make it possible to offer digital copies as open access. Subscription rates: One year: $25; Three years: $65; Five years: $95. You can subscribe to The WAC Journal and pay securely by credit card or PayPal at the Parlor Press website: http://www.parlorpress.com/wacjournal. Or you can send your name, email address, and mailing address along with a check (payable to Parlor Press) to Parlor Press, 3015 Brackenberry Drive, Anderson SC 29621. Email: sales@parlorpress.com

Reproduction of material from this publication, with acknowledgement of the source, is hereby authorized for educational use in non-profit organizations.

The WAC Journal
Volume 25, 2014

Contents

What if the Earth Is Flat? Working With, Not Against,
Faculty Concerns about Grammar in Student Writing   7
Daniel Cole

Disciplining Grammar: A Response to Daniel Cole   36
Joanna Wolfe

Knowing What We Know about Writing in the Disciplines:
A New Approach to Teaching for Transfer in FYC   42
Joanna Wolfe, Barrie Olson, and Laura Wilder

The Connected Curriculum: Designing a Vertical Transfer Writing Curriculum   78
Dan Melzer

Transfer and the Transformation of Writing Pedagogies in a Mathematics Course   92
Sarah Bryant, Noreen Lape, and Jennifer Schaefer

Translation, Transformation, and "Taking it Back":
Moving between Face-to-Face and Online Writing in the Disciplines   106
Heidi Skurat Harris, Tawnya Lubbes, Nancy Knowles, and Jacob Harris

Stephen Wilhoit: A Stealth WAC Practitioner   127
Carol Rutz

The Tables Are Turned: Carol Rutz   136
Terry Myers Zawacki

Review   145
Mya Poe

    Kathleen Blake Yancey, Liane Robertson, and Kara Taczak. *Writing Across Contexts: Transfer, Composition, and Sites of Writing*

Contributors   150

What if the Earth Is Flat? Working With, Not Against, Faculty Concerns about Grammar in Student Writing

DANIEL COLE

One of the biggest and most frustrating divides between writing studies faculty and professors from other disciplines concerns grammar instruction. Many if not all of us in writing across the curriculum (WAC) and/or writing studies have at least one story of encountering an outside colleague (or an upper administrator) and being harangued about the abominable state of student grammar knowledge. The aggrieved colleague might invoke a Golden Age (perhaps when he was an undergraduate) when student writing was not so alarmingly bad. The colleague might also credit her arriving at a successful academic career in part to the hard–nosed grammar mavenry of a past teacher. We try to respond; we offer things about non–expert prose, unfamiliar genres, and the complex interplay between grammar and rhetoric; in other words, we offer elevator–ride versions of Hartwell, Bartholomae, and Joseph Willliams. We might even follow up by emailing the colleague a link to the National Council of Teachers of English (NCTE) web page entitled "Questions and Answers about Grammar."

But these largely causal explanations fail to resonate with the results–oriented colleague. When we escape to safety, we shake our heads. Of course, not all such conversations are unpleasant or even unwelcome, though they can be especially troubling if they carry some degree of subtext concerning the "inadequacies"—limitations, we would say—of first-year composition. Whatever the circumstances, we are always left wondering: how can we help our colleagues better understand and appreciate the myriad factors that contribute to grammar error in student writing? It's like geology faculty routinely having to deal with colleagues who insist the earth is flat.

Or is it? What if we credit our colleagues' perspectives on this issue a bit more? After all, a principle we try to uphold in my institution's WAC program is not to go too far in presenting ourselves as gurus or missionaries of writing, but instead to encourage a free flow of ideas about writing instruction to and from every direction. The primary goal of this essay is to address head–on this grammar divide between writing faculty and cross–disciplinary colleagues. Rather than attempting to disabuse such faculty of their beliefs, it may be more fruitful to listen to their concerns and enlist their aid in developing approaches and resources that address grammar issues in ways that are both positive and pedagogically sound.

The rest of this essay will have four components. First, it will note ways the issue emerges in Toby Fulwiler's essays on running faculty development events. Next, it will relate a tale from the trenches from my own institution; more specifically, it will describe a grammar discussion that took place during and after our faculty writing retreat. Next, it will consider Patrick Hartwell's seminal essay "Grammar, Grammars, and the Teaching of Grammar," whose arguments are the lynchpin of the predominant view that explicit grammar instruction is of prohibitively questionable value. I also examine the response to Hartwell and examine the somewhat marginalized and disjointed state of inquiry into college-level grammar instruction post–Hartwell. Finally, I describe a "Writing List" under development on our campus in response to a discussion that took place at a WAC retreat. Along with the list's genesis, I also explain its premises, potential, and acknowledge its limitations and pitfalls.

Uncovering the Flat Earth

Toby Fulwiler's foundational article "Showing, Not Telling, at a Writing Workshop" is perhaps the best starting point to contextualize how our retreat gave rise to this essay. The passage with particular relevance to the issues I'm undertaking here appear early in the essay under the heading "Workshop 1, Exploring," which opens like this: "Many teachers who attend writing workshops believe, initially at least, that they will learn how to banish forever bad spelling and comma splices from student papers. These teachers are usually disappointed because I teach them no such tricks" (56). In what follows, Fulwiler implies this disappointment does not linger. He describes asking his participants to list "writing problems they perceive as most common, serious, or troublesome." The resulting list, according to Fulwiler, may run up to as many as thirty items. The lists are then subdivided into "fewer, more general categories" such as "1. Motivation 2. Mechanics 3. Style 4. Reading 5. Critical thinking 6. Cognitive maturity 7. Assignments." This exercise is certainly valuable and, I'm sure, often persuasive in providing a more complete sense of the various factors that contribute to grammar error. A practical benefit worth noting is that the exercise would sort out some key definitions, since faculty often have differing senses of what is meant by the term *grammar*. I'd also observe parenthetically that such a list of faculty concerns comprises rich raw material for potential WAC resources.

Fulwiler continues by asserting that, "no participant who helped shape the preceding list can comfortably hold on to the notion that 'spelling or grammar drills' will cure all or most grammar problems." While this may be so, it might also be too dismissive. Consider for a moment that in the list quoted above, grammar is directly invoked in two of the first three items: "Mechanics" and "Style." This persisting emphasis on grammar raises the possibility that Fulwiler's audience might not have changed their mindsets as much as the description implies. Furthermore, complicating or problematizing faculty notions about grammar error, especially if there is no subsequent move into praxis, risks leaving them unable to find ways to accommodate these problems in their pedagogical practices, and risks simply leaving them frustrated. (As will be seen in the next section of this essay, our own retreat participants, though they never advocated drill, certainly retained their concerns with grammar.)

It's worth dwelling for a moment on the fact that we can't always be sure what notions WAC event attendees hold onto once they leave. Deference, compliance, and even enthusiasm are not sure indicators of what they have absorbed, much less what they might put into practice.[1] Fulwiler makes this point himself in his 1984 essay, "How Well Does Writing Across the Curriculum Work?" According to Fulwiler, one place this problem of "translation" can easily emerge is in disciplines with scant tradition of writing in the classroom. In a vivid example, the essay offers an account of a mathematics professor "who seemed to understand theoretically most of what went on at the workshop, [yet] stated later that the only thing he could think to do, practically, was send all his 150 calculus students to tour the writing lab—under penalty of failing the course" (117). Another example involves a forestry professor who, "six months after she attended a workshop and told us how much it meant to her, said that the main things she looks for on papers are 'spelling, style, and neatness.'" Fulwiler adds, "While we don't dismiss these items, her answer dismays us" (118). (Again, I would note the persisting concern with "style," which again raises definition questions, but likely involves concerns with grammar.)

While I can certainly sympathize with Fulwiler's "dismay," I also believe that these faculty and others like them are reminders that we in WAC need to work towards meeting faculty where they are, whether the issue is disciplinary dissonance or skepticism about WAC premises and philosophy. Our charge in WAC is not simply to provide tips and strategies and leave it up to the instructors to adapt them, if they can, to their particular disciplinary contexts. We must also listen to outside faculty, and allow them to take the lead.

Listening to Cross–Disciplinary Faculty

With just under seven thousand undergraduates, our institution is a mid–sized, private university located in a suburb of a major northeastern city. Our WAC program is relatively young, about four years old. We had five faculty development workshops over the course of three semesters under our belt during the events described here, so the two-day faculty writing retreat was the most ambitious event we had yet put on. The retreat was held in our writing center, and we attracted thirteen participants representing a respectable variety of departments: geology, psychology, English, political science, fine arts, philosophy, theater and dance, geography, and a few others.

What made our group perhaps atypical was the number of senior faculty. One was a department chair, and two more became chairs the following academic year. Along with their teaching duties, others were in charge of key campus programs, including our honors college and a program that forms special-interest course clusters for first-year students.

Their varying backgrounds and connections to different student populations coupled with their shared concern for student writing made this group a very nice audience for us. Obviously, they were all experienced instructors; furthermore, their administrative work positioned them to have an interdisciplinary perspective, and, finally, it became very clear as the retreat progressed that they came to the event in an ideal spirit: as instructors with a proactive concern for improving student writing, an openness to reevaluating their pedagogical practices in order to do so, an eagerness to discuss these issues with colleagues, and ultimately a willingness to change their pedagogical practices as a result of the experience. These attributes underpinned a final value of this audience: their candor. Rather than nodding along and going with the flow, our audience did not hesitate to raise questions and challenge our premises. The resulting discussion was both collegial and fully driven by genuine intellectual curiosity and concerns. We did our best to accommodate or suggest correctives, but it became apparent that there were interesting gaps between the retreat participants and the writing studies facilitators in ways of thinking about student writing instruction.

This phenomenon was most acute, and most relevant for the purposes of this essay, in the session devoted to commenting on student work. As it happened, I co-facilitated this segment along with a colleague who is also our department chair. We wanted to convey a few simple ideas that could be summed up as follows: balance positive and negative feedback, and be sure to engage each student individually and intellectually. We had a brief PowerPoint, but the core of the workshop was a student essay for participants to grade on their own and then discuss as a group. We asked participants to consider the various roles they assume in their comments, which might range from critic, to editor, to coach, to that of a co-investigator who takes students' ideas as seriously as she would those of a colleague. We emphasized the latter role especially, which of course led us to deemphasize responding to grammar and sentence-level concerns.

As discussion progressed, attendees increasingly raised the question of grammar errors and how to respond to the student essay on the sentence level. Things reached a point where we as facilitators had to depart significantly from our plan. While the sample student essay definitely had some issues with grammar and style—I had flagged some of them myself—we found ourselves trying to persuade the group that these errors were not the optimum focal point for comments directed to the student.

We attempted to introduce the categories of "global" and "local" concerns. We tried to demonstrate that many of the local issues were related to the student's grappling with a complex topic (hydraulic fracturing, or fracking). I also pointed out that the student's tendency toward agent-less syntax was to some degree standard in the field he was training for (he belonged to a composition section devoted to first-year engineering majors). In another phase of the discussion, we invoked Nancy Sommers's point that we put students at cross-purposes with themselves if we ask them to adjust a sentence on the one hand, while also asking them to rethink or even remove the paragraph it is located in. From a writing studies perspective, we gave the "right" orthodox answers, but many in our audience didn't buy it.

Something of a paradox came into play. They often said either implicitly or explicitly, "You're the experts; you tell us." For our part, we were in fact speaking from our expertise; we even offered bibliography for just about everything we were saying (in addition, a copy of John Bean's *Engaging Ideas* was given to each attendee at the outset of the retreat). Still, what we were saying was just too much at odds with how the attendees themselves conceptualized and practiced writing instruction and development. It seemed they simply could not get their minds around experts in writing pedagogy telling them to deemphasize grammar. Perhaps they felt as though they were encountering geologists who were insisting the earth is flat.

Joking aside, attendees are certainly justified in asking for rock-solid praxis they could immediately use on the ground. We thought we were giving them that, of course, but clearly we were off target with their most pressing concerns. Obviously, this troubled my co-facilitator and me. We wondered if we should have been more prepared to confront this issue; maybe we blew an opportunity. We also were a bit surprised because both of us had facilitated faculty development events on feedback before without this issue coming so urgently to the fore. It soon became clear, however, that little we could have said or done in those immediate circumstances would have been likely to change their mindsets.

Soon after the retreat, we asked them via email to reply and describe their experience, including any takeaways they valued, along with constructive input they may have to guide us as we plan future events. Nearly all of them replied with well-thought-out responses to both facets of the question. Their answers did in fact balance positive and negative feedback, so we may have been successful there. More importantly, the replies were candid and incredibly eye-opening in suggesting how deep the gap between writing and non-writing faculty may be, especially in terms of sentence-level pedagogies.

An art history professor wrote, "I finished the workshop feeling I am at odds with many of the writing pedagogies that are currently popular" in writing studies. For her, this feeling was most pronounced on the issue of grammar, and our discipline's general commitment to process theory which endeavors to improve student writing by encouraging several stages of revision that move from "global" or "higher order" issues "down" to low-order issues. This professor strongly disagreed with this concept, and argued that students should instead be trained to write from the sentence level up:

> We spent very little (if any) time talking about specific ways to improve student sentences. I am of the opinion that without sound sentences, all the revisions in the world won't lead to better writing. Without strong sentences, there can be no clarity in writing, and without clarity in writing, there's no clarity in thinking (something mentioned during one of the presentations). Unfortunately, for reasons I do not understand, students no longer arrive in college able to write strong sentences. Nothing I learned in the workshop made me change my mind that strong writing begins with the foundation of strong sentences, and I wish there had been more talk about this problem.

She also suggested a different approach to the sample student paper: "I would like to have heard [the facilitators] talk us through the paper—first an overview than a line-by-line study followed by an example of a good first revision, and then a final draft."

More attendees echoed this model-oriented proposal. A philosophy professor said, "It would be great to watch the writing studies faculty mark up a paper they're seeing for the first time—just to see how you approach it and what you say. Then we talk [. . .] in detail about why you made this or that comment." Attendees would then try commenting on a paper themselves in light of the discussion. The participant added: "I had imagined that's what we would be doing. I do understand (really I do) that, compared to what you guys are thinking about, that's not terribly interesting. Still."

Another professor expressed a similar desire simply to see "the feedback given by an experienced writing instructor to the student on each of [several sequential] drafts." Though one might say this attendee, and the one quoted above, might assume too much homogeneity among writing studies faculty, it is important to look past this problem and see that these participants are rightly eager to find something to hang their hat on. This desire comes across vividly, along with an implied primary concern with sentence-level issues, in this commentary from a psychology professor: "I have an implicit sense of what clear prose requires, but I have no formal training in teaching the craft of writing. It's likely that I spend far too much time correcting student papers because I do not know how to spot errors quickly and how to respond effectively and with greater efficiency."

Yet another participant came to our presentation with a very open mind, but found little of practical use:

> I admit to hoping I would be told that the way I write comments and corrections on papers is all wrong because it is ineffective. I wanted you to tell me that because I have a sense that it is ineffective but I'm not certain. When I look back over the two days, I can't say with any certainty that I've got new tools for that aspect of my writing instruction practice. [...] Of course, I realize that there is more to writing instruction than correcting papers. But to be honest, correcting papers is where I end up spending the vast majority of my time. While I will take advantage of some of the tips given to help my students get off to a better start when it comes to completing my writing assignments, it doesn't feel like the way I grade them will change much, if at all.

This of course is the opposite of what we were hoping for.

This attendee's words raise the fraught question Fulwiler grapples with: how can we know the extent to which our faculty development events are resulting in changed practices on the part of instructors, and furthermore, improved writing on the part of students? Moreover, how can we ensure that what emerges from workshops are pedagogical models that can be adapted and implemented—recall Fulwiler's calculus and forestry professors—in a variety of classroom contexts ("How Well" 118).

Something very heartening, however, about all of the attendee feedback was that they demonstrated a willingness to take on a substantial measure of responsibility for grammar instruction. Throughout the retreat, attendees found many occasions to voice the need for a "common language" about writing that faculty across disciplines could share with students, and thereby mutually reinforce writing instruction. Again, we thought that's what we were providing, or at least moving toward, but it somehow didn't gain purchase.

The notion of "common language" emerged again and again in the post–retreat written feedback. One attendee bridged the idea with oft-suggested "line-by-line" workshop:

> I didn't get a good sense of a "common" [Writing Studies] or WAC vocabulary. [...] I think it would be helpful to provide participants with much more specific, concrete examples, work through examples of editing and giving comments on student papers using that vocabulary, and to perhaps develop an outline that identifies frequent mistakes or issues and that helps faculty develop and work with a common vocabulary for talking with students about their papers. Most students will go to their specific instructors

about a paper, so if a goal of WAC is to develop such a common vocabulary, then it would be good to have a concrete, specific guide as to what that is.

Another participant put it this way:

> I would have liked to spend some time on a review of common writing errors, and how to deal with these errors when we see them in student writing. It would be helpful to see a list of features of student writing that we can point out to students in an encouraging way to reinforce good writing practices.

In a similar vein, another remarked:

> I think learning a little bit of grammar (around 15 general "rules," spelled out with 2 or 3 examples) leads almost every student to write better sentences. (Writing better paragraphs, organizing those paragraphs, and developing a thesis are another matter, and I found [Bean's *Engaging Ideas*], as well as some of the workshop tips, offered several good pointers on this front.) [. . .]
>
> I think for WAC to work, the program needs to come up with an agreed–upon basic vocabulary. Students should move from class to class knowing basic editing marks, understanding a sentence requires a subject and a predicate, etc. (my pet peeves)–along with whatever you think is necessary.

The recurrence of the grammar list idea was one reason it was hard to dismiss.

A more important reason was that the idea held promise. We became convinced such a resource could provide a valuable, campus–wide reference point for talking about grammar and writing. A geology professor who advocated this idea pulled it all into focus in this way:

> I think that the best thing that could come out of a WAC program would be a set of common teaching strategies, vocabularies for writing skills, expectations for what constitutes acceptable writing, and tools made available to students. If every instructor insists on grammatically correct sentences in student writing, makes that expectation upfront and explicit, and sends students to the same resources for help (e.g., OWL, Writing Center) and if we all give them the same handout at the beginning of the semester on the need for essays to have a thesis statement, supporting evidence, and a properly formatted bibliography, eventually they will catch on. I'm talking about very

minimal stuff–the baseline. Developing this sort of common writing toolkit would be a good task for a future multidisciplinary workshop.

A toolkit, a grammar list, and a writing list—such things would not be a panacea, and they would certainly have their drawbacks, but they would have some positive advantages.

First, retreat participant commentary suggested to us that more faculty members might be likely to buy into WAC if there were simple resources like this. A ten to fifteen item list would quickly give faculty who lacked one a grammar vocabulary. Moreover, sentence-level commenting could be done with greater efficiency, a prospect that would no doubt be attractive to many faculty members. Furthermore, recall the grammar conversation scenario that opened this essay; as writing faculty in those situations, we could simply refer interlocutors to the list, and offer our open door through email for comments and questions. For students, the list could be an accessible starting point, more digestible, perhaps, than a grammar textbook or an extensive grammar website.

But devising such a list is not as simple as it may seem. The fact that our list would be developed in response to explicit requests from faculty across the university helped us avoid the pitfall of its being suspiciously regarded by faculty across campus as a unilateral document or a Trojan horse of some kind. Even so, there remains the problem that the list might all too readily lend itself to heavy-handed prescriptivism, a sort of Ten Commandments of Writing, which is an impression we would want to avoid. In other words, we would not want the list to function or come to be adopted as a rigid set of standards, but rather as tool or guide, a simple, common reference point for talking about writing in terms of grammar. But how does one reach that goal? How long should the list be? How long should entries be? Which issues should be included? What kind of examples and explanations would work best? Besides these practical concerns, there is also the need to make the list theoretically and pedagogically sound. How might the list accurately reflect the place of grammar on the landscape of writing and writing instruction? The following section will engage these theoretical and pedagogical concerns. The subsequent section will explore the practical issues.

Hartwell in Context and in Content

Since this essay advocates greater attention to grammar in our WAC programs, classrooms and scholarly discussions, it is important to more closely examine the arguments that underpin skepticism in our field about grammar instruction. The touchstone text for this position remains Patrick Hartwell's "Grammar, Grammars, and the Teaching of Grammar" which argues that writing students will be blocked or impeded if we preoccupy them with the mechanical workings of grammar as they write. A key point for Hartwell is that the term *grammar* tends to be used too loosely. In a frequently referenced schema, he enumerates five senses of the word ranging from intuitive grammar knowledge held by native speakers (Grammar 1), through linguistics (Grammar 2) to the grammar of standard etiquette (Grammar 3), textbook grammar (Grammar 4), and finally style (Grammar 5). The essence of Hartwell's argument is that explicit instruction of Grammar 3, 4, or 5, especially in the form of drill, disrupts the operations of Grammar 1, which stem from our deeply ingrained language instinct and are thus paramount. At best, writes Hartwell, such grammar instruction is "COIK," Clear Only If Known—in other words, textbook grammar explanations tend to be laden with grammar jargon, thereby falsely assuming an audience that already has some expertise, a phenomenon likely to frustrate student and novice writers.

This foundational essay is approaching its fourth decade of being central to the grammar question; furthermore, the empirical data on grammar drill that plays a key role in Hartwell's argument is now fifty years old. These facts alone might suggest the essay may be due for reconsideration, not necessarily to discredit it, but rather to see what it can tell us today. Though the essay still plays a central role in our thinking, it is also important to situate it in its initial context. In a significant sense, it participates in a particular moment in the debate over formal grammar instruction that seems especially fraught, so heated in fact that Hartwell notes how it has been characterized by name-calling, and he also suggests with evident frustration that further empirical work would not settle anything but instead be cancelled out by confirmation biases (107).

While the essay is generally regarded as settling, to some extent, the question of whether grammar should be taught at the university-level—and that is indeed the larger question Hartwell engages at the opening of his essay—it also seems to suggest that question is at an impasse, and ultimately situates its argument in response to a much narrower question. Consider how he describes the model of instruction he is critiquing, (one that, incidentally fits the "sentence-up" approach advocated by one of our retreat attendees), and his role in that debate:

> I want to focus on the notion of [instructional] sequence that makes the grammar issue so important: first grammar, then usage, then some absolute model of organization, all controlled by the teacher at the center of the learning process, with other matters [. . .] pushed off to the future. It is not surprising that we call each other names: those of us who question the value of teaching grammar are in fact shaking the whole elaborate edifice of traditional composition instruction. (109)

Some may reasonably see the image of the controlling teacher as crucial here; the counterpoint to that image may be Peter Elbow's *Writing Without Teachers*. This zero-sum formulation might be positively resolved by Paulo Freire's "problem-posing" educator in *Pedagogy of the Oppressed*. Another key part of this passage is the critical role that the question of "sequence" holds in Hartwell's argument. Indeed, approaching the essay with this awareness reveals that Hartwell's argument actually addresses itself less to whether grammar instruction should be practiced in the writing classroom, and more to the narrower point that grammar should not be the starting point of writing instruction.

My point here is that we must reread Hartwell's argument while bearing in mind his stated aim of dislodging a pedagogy that uses sentence-level grammar as its starting point. Given that Hartwell frames his argument this way, citing his essay in today's pedagogical context as an authoritative justification for ignoring or de-emphasizing grammar instruction is to repurpose the article, and possibly ask it to carry more weight than it can bear.

Becky L. Caouette has also argued that it is time to take another look at Hartwell's essay. She notes that "Grammar, Grammars, and the Teaching of Grammar" is "the most widely reprinted article in Composition," especially in anthologies aimed at "Composition instructors [either] new or experienced" (57). Despite this ubiquity, writes Caouette, "no real critical attention" has been paid to Hartwell's article since a brief response that appeared in *College English* in 1986 (57). Caouette observes, "the critical invisibility of the text seems at odds with its pervasiveness in anthologies" (57). This discrepancy, argues Caouette, poses a problem with serious ramifications for the field of Composition:

> This complete absence of critical reflection intrigues me, particularly considering the fact that we are repeatedly asking newcomers to the field—teachers and scholars—to examine this text in the anthologies we provide. Yet as a field we have not returned to it ourselves in any substantial way. Thus we run the risk of repeating old mistakes, of misrepresenting our current stances or the debates that frame our work, or of sending incomplete, or even erroneous messages to the next generation. We simply insert "Grammar" in our anthologies in an effort to avoid revising that chapter of our history—one that might look very different through our current theoretical, historical, and pedagogical lenses. (58)

I would add that the problems Caouette identifies have especially acute consequences for those of us in WAC who must address this issue with colleagues outside the field. The state of the grammar question post-Hartwell leaves us in an awkward, difficult to explain position partially because Hartwell's argument defies easy summary for an outsider audience. In other words, to revisit this essay's opening scenario, we're left trying to sell a difficult proposition—we seem to be saying the earth is flat—rather than offering a positive response. The missed opportunity here lies in the fact that the true grammar discrepancy between writing faculty and professors in the disciplines is more one of proportion. We see grammar as a comparatively narrow slice of the writing pie; they see a larger slice—some, of course, think it's the whole pie.

I should pause for a moment, however, and point out that Caouette is too absolutist in her picture of our field's relationship to grammar. There have been many worthy attempts to advance discourse on grammar instruction at the college level in a post–Hartwell world. In 1991, Rei Noguchi published a book that both critiqued the bedrock studies Hartwell cited and offered a way forward for college grammar instruction. Four years later, Susan Hunter and Ray Wallace edited an anthology of essays that pursued these same goals.[2] In 1996, *College English*, the journal where "Grammars" appeared the decade before, ran a special issue on grammar instruction. Unfortunately, these very fine efforts failed to ignite further discussion. The next signpost did not appear until a 2002 article by Bonnie Devet, which offered three approaches to reconcile grammar instruction with process pedagogies. This essay was followed in 2004 by Laura Micciche's "Making the Case for Rhetorical Grammar." Like Caouette, Micciche notes an "absence of sustained contemporary conversation about grammar instruction at the college level" which is at odds, she argues, with the need to teach students "to communicate effectively" (717). Although Micciche lists "Grammars" in her works cited, she does not engage Hartwell directly. Instead, her argument engages political objections to grammar instruction (which this essay will also briefly take up below). This article is regarded in the field as a landmark statement on productive grammar instruction, especially in the strain of composition concerned with civic engagement and socio–cultural critique.

A decade on from Micciche's essay, Caouette's interrogative conclusion offers a provocative statement of the field's current relationship to grammar:

> Do we [anthologize Hartwell] so that we can avoid talking about grammar issues with others, and thereby preemptively dismiss criticism about the absence of traditional grammar instruction in Composition classrooms? Is it an unwillingness to engage in continued inquiry in the field, even if, as [Chris] Anson (2008) argued, that inquiry is necessary—that new questions are emerging? Is it possible that the message Hartwell conveyed—that traditional grammar instruction as we knew it has no place in the modern classroom—is a dated argument that we nevertheless continue to promulgate [. . .]? Such questions that have not been answered elsewhere, point, I argue, to Composition's unease with this topic on the college level and with

our desire to present one article, one perspective, as the definitive one in the field. (61)

Though I understand why Caouette asks these questions, I would probably answer no to them, albeit not emphatically. Though I agree that the field has ground to make up in this regard, I would not say that this state of affairs amounts to a willful avoidance of grammar issues. Certain signs point to possibly different state of affairs when it comes to actual classroom practice. A significant number of writing instructors apparently do in fact find a place for grammar in their curriculum. They flag comma splices; they assign grammar texts; they refer students to the Purdue Online Writing Lab (OWL) (which seems to be thriving); they likely do many other things in class and in consultations. Clearly, grammar instruction has not been abandoned. It simply seems circumscribed within the classroom.

To take a step out of that circle, I would propose we begin by examining the immediate responses to Hartwell's essay by Martha Kolln and others. A close revisiting of certain particulars of that discussion and how the debate played out combined to produce the strange result Caouette addresses: a canonical scholarly article that left scant discussion in its wake. In what follows, I will attempt to show that this lack of critical engagement may be owing in part to the multi-faceted nature of Hartwell's argument, but also, and more importantly, to the initial intensity of the debate, which had the unfortunate result of distorting general impressions of its outcome, and obscuring an apparent consensus that grammar taught rhetorically or in context was—and continues to be—a promising way forward.

The immediate responses to Hartwell's article were rigorous, impassioned, and, as we know, ultimately ineffectual in undermining the essay. The first wave appeared with four reactions to Hartwell in the "Comment and Response" section of *College English*'s October 1985 issue. In the following December issue of the journal, yet another comment appeared by Hartwell's most prominent nemesis, Martha Kolln. One striking element of the exchange is a level of strong and emotionally charged language relatively unusual in a published academic debate. Edward Vavra opens his commentary rather aggressively: "'COIK'? 'Worship'? 'Incantations'? Patrick Hartwell should make up his mind. Either he has written a rational argument against the teaching of grammar or he is playing on our emotions" (647). Richard D. Cureton accuses Hartwell of deploying "sloppy examples," and calls his sample grammatical analyses "disturbingly naïve" (646, 645). Kolln insists, "You're wrong about me, Professor Hartwell. I am quite willing to put to rest the issue of 'formal grammar'" (875). Hartwell retorts that, "Professor Kolln is flat out wrong" on several points (878). Indeed, he opens his reply to Kolln somewhat dismissively: "There's little to be accomplished by talking across paradigms, so I'll try to be brief about this" (877). Hartwell also sees something suspicious in the shifting referents in Kolln's use of the pronoun "we," which range between members of the field generally and those who agree or disagree with her. Hartwell remarks accusingly, "We can see what's going on here" (878).

It should not be ignored, however, that Hartwell's critics raised legitimate concerns. In fact, one reason there had been no subsequent re-evaluation of Hartwell is that, for the most part, one could only elaborate on these initial critiques. Kolln and others pointed to soft spots, inconsistencies, and unclear definitions in key studies that served as a lynchpin for Hartwell. Carol Moses expresses concern about the implications of Hartwell's argument for basic writers; further, she suggests that Hartwell misrepresents Mina Shaugnessy as being opposed to teaching grammar, and notes Hartwell's "selective" examples (which were rooted in particularly intuitive aspects of grammar, such as article use and the order of cumulative adjectives) (645–46). Vavra also remarks on Hartwell's skewed examples, and argues that Hartwell makes a misleading appeal to Noam Chomsky. In addition, Vavra and Cureton both find Hartwell's linguistic theoretical grounding incomplete. As we know, these objections did not suffice, and Hartwell's article remains the most influential treatment of the issue.[3]

This outcome is probably not surprising. Advocates of grammar instruction faced an all but insurmountable obstacle in the empirical studies arrayed against them. One can raise questions about method, definitions, and semantics, but generally speaking, such arguments rarely seem to gain traction; it seems simpler for those who are undecided simply to trust the science. On the whole, it seems that studies can only be persuasively refuted by other studies. Another problem for the pro-grammar side was (and is) comprised in the principle that getting people to take action is generally more difficult than getting people to take no action; it may be more precise to say it is quite difficult to persuade people to act against their inclinations. While many in our field do incorporate grammar instruction, many do not. It is no doubt seductive or convenient to have an authoritative license to ignore or deemphasize grammar in favor of focusing more on literary or content analysis. As decades elapse with inconsistent and unstable grammar instruction, few will be inclined to fill gaps in their knowledge of grammatical terminology and analysis. Still, this trend may yet be reversed.

The bitter tone of the debate surrounding Hartwell's article belies an apparent and considerable common ground. Cureton writes, "I have no problem with Hartwell's thesis" (643). Moses objects to "grammar as taught by most textbooks" (645). Vavra asserts that "much of the grammar that is currently taught is not only a waste of time but also harmful in that it bores and frustrates students" (647). Even Kolln writes, "I agree with [Hartwell...] that formal method is certainly not the way to teach grammar" (875). Despite his assertion that he was "talking across paradigms," Hartwell avers, "if Kolln and I were to agree to examine carefully what passes for writing instruction in American classrooms—from kindergarten through college—we'd find it dripping with a kind of grammar instruction we'd both deplore" (877, 878). Hartwell also concedes, "I would agree with all the respondents that a knowledge of the English language and a vocabulary for discussing style are useful attainments for literate adults" (649).

With all of this consensus, why was the dispute so heated? One could speculate about answers to that question, but unfortunately, this situation seems to be an example of a debate creating more heat than light. Adding to this misfortune, the vehemence on both sides seems to have created a lasting impression that the two positions were further apart and more antithetical than they really were. In other words, a simplistic narrative appears to have emerged: there was an intense debate over grammar instruction, and the anti–grammar side won. Such an impression might have been confirmed for any professor (from any discipline) who merely glanced at the headline for a 2003 article by Dennis Baron in the *Chronicle of Higher Education*: "Teaching Grammar Doesn't Lead to Better Writing." While that statement seemed to be the takeaway when the dust settled, the real question at the heart of the matter was not whether grammar should be taught, but how it should be taught.

That issue was foregrounded by one of Hartwell's respondents whom I have not yet mentioned. Joseph Williams offers a response which stands out from the others because he does not offer any critique whatsoever of Hartwell's argument. Instead, Williams focuses on how to proceed given that formal grammar instruction had apparently been discredited. Leaving aside the issue of grammar instruction in primary and secondary schools, Williams postulates, "Mature writers—past age 20, say—profit from powerful generalizations about style." Williams further argues that grammar instruction should "synthesize information from all grammars available, plus whatever information other theories of language might provide." This approach to grammar would produce "*a vocabulary crucial to talking about style,* not just to teach our students to write clearly, but so that they can talk to others about the writing of those others" (642, emphasis in original). Williams was also alone in receiving an entirely positive reaction from Hartwell, who observes that Williams's insights are "suggestive about how we might articulate what we know about writing to our students" (649).

For the significant number of people who continued (and continue) to teach grammar on the college level after these debates, Williams's guidebook, *Style: Lessons in Clarity and Grace*, in its tenth edition as of this writing, has been a useful resource. Likewise, Martha Kolln's *Rhetorical Grammar* offers an approach to grammar instruction that both easily integrates with student writing, and equips students to read more effectively with attention to the rhetorical effects of grammatical choices.

I'd like to focus on Williams for a moment because his philosophy underpins the writing list that we're devising in our WAC program in conjunction with our writing center in response to retreat attendees' request for such an artifact.

The Writing List's Premises and Rationale

A list of common grammar or stylistic issues might seem simple to compile, but in fact there are a number of practical pedagogical considerations to balance. Since Williams's assertion that college writing students are capable of absorbing and applying general principles provides the pedagogical foundation to the writing list we devised, Williams's own lists on the inside covers of *Style* became one key starting point. Thus, our own list was conceived as an enumeration of both useful principles related to style, but given our retreat faculty's concerns, I also wanted to accommodate common student grammatical errors. Tabulations of grammar errors in college-student writing have at least a 100-year history. In 1988, Robert Connors and Andrea Lunsford noted that devising lists of common student writing errors had been practiced toward various ends since at least 1910 (397). Connors and Lunsford generated their own list of the "top twenty" errors in student writing; that effort was replicated twenty years later by Andrea Lunsford and Karen Lunsford (403; 795). Another touchstone deserving mention is Maxine Hairston's 1981 charting of reactions to particular writing errors as registered by a large cross section of professionals for whom students might conceivably write beyond college.

Though it is based on unscientific observation of student writing, our list turns out to align more or less favorably with Connors and Lunsford's list. Our list covers three of their top five, as well as five of the top ten items listed in order of English teachers' concerns, that is, the "rank of # of errors marked by teacher" (403). Similarly, our list includes two of the top three errors judged by professionals in Hairston's classification (as charted by Noguchi) to be "very serious," and two of the top four listed as "serious" (Noguchi 25). Our list also compares reasonably well to Lunsford and Lunsford's revised list from 2008. There is an overlap comprising two of the top four, and overall, we share eight of twenty items.

I would like to have meshed a bit more closely, but I would account for this twelve-point gap in three ways. To begin, four of those errors—involving diction, spelling, capitalization, and missing words—I judged inappropriate for our list because they were either too essay-specific (in the case of diction) or more likely to result from inattention (in the case of our student population at least) than ignorance of the grammatical or stylistic principles involved. Second, Lunsford and Lunsford encountered three additional errors that stemmed from documentation and quotation integration. I deemed such issues to be too discipline-specific to be generalized on our list. For a time, we included a statement that read in effect, "Check with your professor to ensure proper quotation integration and documentation of sources." I removed this statement for being too vague, and more importantly because I believe that the onus should be on professors to make such issues clear to students rather than professors waiting for students to raise them, or figure them out on their own. Finally, Lunsford and Lunsford's list focuses on errors in strictly formal grammar, and I wanted our list to also include stylistic concerns such as smooth sentence-level transitions, effective use of passive voice, and similar issues.

The general aim for this document is to provide a clear and contained list of principles to help students and faculty alike build grammar and stylistic awareness based upon a common vocabulary. I envision the list emerging through grass-roots (it's emanation from a cross-faculty retreat is a crucial element, it should be stressed) and working primarily as a reference point that could be incorporated into feedback on student work. When professors encounter grammar issues in a student's paper—a run-on sentence, for example—they could simply refer students to the list: "See list #4" or words to that effect; a professor who grades electronically could provide a link if the list is on-line. I see this resource as especially useful for instructors who value and have an intuitive sense of appropriate grammar application, but perhaps lack a means or vocabulary to convey these issues to students. Such persons might acquaint themselves with the list over a cup of coffee, and grow increasingly familiar with it with use over time. A student might do the same, of course. Ideally, the number of professors using the list would snowball, and a typical student might then encounter and use the list in multiple classes, increasing the student's likelihood of internalizing it. In other words, the list might aim at the same goals the many institutions hope to achieve with common grammar textbooks, but with the advantage of a more digestible, approachable format.

To increase the likelihood the scenarios described above might be realized, it was crucial that the list's explanations effectively balance concision and completeness. This premise also underlies Noguchi's approach to grammar instruction, which emphasizes both succinctness, and working with grammar knowledge students may already intuitively hold (34). Another concern taken into account is Hartwell's COIK observation, the idea that textbook grammar explanations tend to be clear only if known, that is, jargon-laden and thus unclear to novices or the uninitiated. This concern also necessitated limiting, but not eliminating, grammar terminology. The trick then is to provide an explanation of a grammatical or stylistic issue that would be adequate for someone approaching it with little or no prior knowledge to gain understanding. The link to the Purdue OWL—which tends to have thorough explanations—would be there to cover any shortfalls. A final guiding principle in designing the list was to eschew bland examples in favor of examples that resemble what students may actually write for class; this of course was another area to avoid the COIK phenomenon.

As an example of handling the concerns listed above, consider the following entry for dangling modifiers:

Fix Dangling and Disruptive Modifiers

> Make sure modifiers match up to the appropriate term. Here's a dangling modifier:
>
> —Claiming dozens of victims every day, doctors worked to contain the epidemic.
>
> (This syntax suggests the doctors are claiming victims.)
>
> To fix the problem, simply rephrase to reflect the logical connections:
>
> —Claiming dozens of victims a day, the epidemic posed a serious challenge for the doctors.
>
> OR
>
> —The doctors worked to contain the epidemic, which claimed dozens of victims a day.
>
> Here's a misplaced, or disruptive modifier:
>
> —Historians have debated whether Queen Elizabeth the First was a virgin for centuries.
>
> To correct, simply straighten out the logic:
>
> —Historians have debated for centuries whether Queen Elizabeth the First was a virgin.

Read more about modifier issues here: https://owl.english.purdue.edu/engagement/2/1/36/

The emphasis on using simple logic to correct the sentences is meant to harness students' intuitive sense of sentence clarity or grammatical correctness. This is also true of the reference to "disruptive" modifiers, which are indicated as being synonymous to the more standard term, misplaced modifier.

Using student intuition about writing as an entry point toward a grammar vocabulary also underpins the following entry:

Ensure that Sentences are Neither Choppy, Nor Rambling

Conjunctions can remedy both choppy writing (by combining sentences), and rambling sentences (by clarifying the relationships between ideas.)

Subordinating conjunctions (unless, until, as, as if, though, although, even though, when, that, than, before, after, while, since, because, so that) create subordinate clauses that both set up and give emphasis to the main clause.

—Although her argument was strong, I was not persuaded.

(Here, the idea of not being persuaded in the main part of the sentence is emphasized more than the idea in the subordinate clause of the argument being strong. Reversing the arrangement would reverse the effect.)

Coordinating conjunctions (for, and, nor, but, or, yet, so) give equal emphasis to two ideas, both of which could stand alone as a sentence:

—I agreed with her thesis, but I thought her evidence was weak.

(Here, the ideas of agreeing with the thesis and the weakness of the evidence are given equal emphasis by the co–ordinate conjunction "but.")

Note: In general, try not to have more than two or three clauses in a single sentence.

Read more about coordination and subordination here: https://owl.english.purdue.edu/engagement/2/1/37/

Though "rambling" and "choppy" may be imprecise terms, they are accessible for novice writers, who may then be guided to an appropriate grammatical terminology about those problems. Rambling sentences? Well, the problem is likely to be ineffective coordination. Choppy sentences? Which of those ideas could be subordinated to others?

Readers may quibble or object as to the degree to which these entries conform to the ideals laid out above (balancing completeness with concision; limiting, but not eliminating, grammar terminology, etc.), but I would welcome that. In presenting the list to my colleagues, I emphasized that everything was fully fungible. I'd say the same to readers of this essay, who surely could produce entries as good or better than these.

I hope I have persuasively demonstrated that the list approach holds pedagogical value and potential, but one thing I cannot promise at this point is that this list approach will be successful. The potential paradox here is that increased grammar knowledge might clarify thinking and talking about writing, but it is by no means certain that this practice would lead to drastic improvements in student writing itself. Perhaps the studies of half a century ago that discredited grammar drill could be replicated or built upon, but it seems likely that it will again prove difficult or impossible to establish a clearly linear causal relationship between grammar instruction and writing improvement. This exchange from Plato's *Gorgias* offers an insight on the slippery nature of grammar instruction:

Socrates: Well, and is not he who has learned carpentering a carpenter?

Gorgias: Yes.

Socrates: And he who has learned music a musician?

Gorgias: Yes.

Socrates: And he who has learned medicine is a physician, in like manner? He who has learned anything whatever is that which his knowledge makes him.

Gorgias: Certainly.

Socrates: And in the same way, he who has learned what is just is just?

Gorgias: To be sure.

We perhaps fall into the same trap Gorgias stumbled into if we try to isolate any direct impact of grammar instruction on student writing, (or of WAC workshops on faculty teaching, for that matter). Our attendees may be in this trap as well since they seem to assume that one who has learned grammar is a good writer. We laborers in WAC must still work to bring to our colleagues our field's findings on grammar error.

This, of course, is not to circle back to the position that grammar instruction is necessarily fruitless, but rather to recognize and keep sight of the oblique relationship between teaching and learning. What if we try to place writing somewhere in the continuum suggested by Socrates's series of examples? Like justice, writing has elements that are intangible and abstract that might be best discerned in examples and models. But writing is also like carpentry and music in that there are certainly technical aspects that are helpful if not necessary to apprehend; basic principles are carried into practice, and progress toward mastery comes through practical immersion and experience. We could probably add many more examples to carpentry, music, and medicine, but we would be hard-put to find many more areas of teaching and learning besides composition that did not give a prominent place to each portion of its technical elements. Surely it is time to find a more conspicuous and productive place for grammar instruction in our writing pedagogy.

Grammar and Politics

Before closing this essay, I want to acknowledge the political dimension of grammar. Many in our field are justifiably concerned that grammar instruction might explicitly or implicitly promote the notion that one version of English among many might be established as "proper" or "standard," thereby marginalizing a great majority of both native and non-native speakers of English. This consideration underpins the NCTE's Statement on Students' Right to Their Own Language. Mike Rose's book *Lives on the Boundary* is perhaps our most eloquent elaboration on how a rigid approach to grammar can devalue, demoralize, and discourage students. In response to the notion of grammar as a potential tool of oppression, Laura Micciche has sought to "challenge those associations" between grammar and the reinforcement of social hierarchies. Micciche argues that a rhetorical approach to grammar instruction can actually empower students, an aim in line with "composition's goals to equip students to be active citizens of the world they inhabit" (733).

Though the factors she refers to may be more than "associations," that does not preclude the empowering conception of grammar instruction that she envisions. The language rights terrain has shifted since the mid-1980's. Around that time, writers such as N'Gugi Wa Thiong' O endeavored to de-colonize their minds by renouncing European languages and embracing those of their cultures, but this attitude has evolved. Today, the literary landscape is much more diverse; we can now hear arguments, ideas, and stories from writers with roots in a broad array of cultures—many of which continue to be impacted by oppression—precisely because these writers are willing to employ standardized grammar to some degree, even as they re-shape the language in other respects. The same can be true for our students; they too should be able to include the meta-language of grammar in their box of rhetorical and analytical tools, enabling them to both understand and be understood.

The idea that grammar knowledge provides access to the public square is not new, of course. Amid a vigorous defense of the value of grammar instruction in the face of an existential threat, John of Salisbury argued in 1159 that grammar is a shared, inclusive public resource that both empowers and protects all who avail themselves of it: "The art [of grammar] is, as it were, a public highway, on which all have the right to journey, walk, and act, immune from criticism and molestation" (54). Viewed in this way, grammar is not inevitably a means of oppression; it is, on the contrary a useful public trust that facilitates a free exchange of ideas and expression. Why should students be denied the use of this resource?

Conclusion

This essay has been something of a winding road, and I will try to consolidate everything here. My largest goal has been to move toward bridging the considerable gap that exists on many campuses between writing faculty and our colleagues in other disciplines when it comes to grammar in student writing. I have argued that it is high time for our field to bring its discussions of grammar pedagogy out of the margins, and reconsider how grammar instruction might be optimally reintegrated into our classrooms.

I think this shift is especially important for those of us in WAC who thus far have generally been less comfortable and less successful than we might care to admit (even to ourselves) in discussing grammar with outside colleagues. Though a common belief among many professors holds that writing instruction is primarily the responsibility of the English or writing department, this attitude may shift if we provide simple, self-contained ways that professors in the disciplines can reinforce and corroborate concepts taught in composition classrooms. Not only that, but we must also listen carefully to cross-disciplinary colleagues rather than viewing them as naïfs who must be disabused of their misconceptions. On our campus, this approach enabled us to produce at least two artifacts that I hope will prove useful: the writing list and this essay. Listening can no doubt lead to useful artifacts on other campuses as well. I look forward to hearing and reading about them.

Acknowledgments

I would like to thank Dr. Frank Gaughan, Dr. Lisa Dresner, and the anonymous reviewers of The WAC Journal for their insights and guidance.

Notes

1. See Swilky for further discussion of "faculty resistance to writing reform," and the opportunities such reactions present. Many studies have looked at WAC program influences on faculty instructional practices. For an overview, see Bazerman 50–53.

2. This volume includes a qualitative study by Donald Bushman and Elizabeth Ervin on instructor responses to grammar in writing in the disciplines (WID) courses. They include among their findings that many of these faculty members were uncertain about responding to grammar issues, and desired resources to that end. See especially pp. 147–50, and 154.

3. *College English* published a final "Comment" in response to "Grammars" in April 1986. Thomas Huckin objected that a grammar exercise he devised was misused and misrepresented in the essay.

Works Cited

Anson, Chris. "The Intelligent Design of Writing Programs: Reliance On Belief Or a Future of Evidence?" *WPA: Writing Program Administration* 32 .1 (Fall 2008): 11–38. Print.

Bartholomae, David. "Inventing the University." *When a Writer Can't Write: Studies in Writer's Block and Other Composing Process Problems*. Ed. Mike Rose. New York: Guildford, 1985. 134–36. Print.

Baron, Dennis. "Teaching Grammar Doesn't Lead to Better Writing." *Chronicle of Higher Education*. (May 16, 2003): B20. Print.

Bushman, Donald, and Elizabeth Ervin. "Rhetorical Contexts of Grammar: Some Views from Writing Emphasis Course Instructors." *The Place of Grammar in Writing Instruction: Past, Present, Future*. Ed. Susan Hunter and Ray Wallace. Portsmouth: Boynton/Cook, 1995: 136–58. Print.

Bazerman, Charles, et al. *Reference Guide to Writing Across the Curriculum*. West Lafayette, IN: Parlor, 2005. Print.

Caouette, Becky L. "On the College Front: Patrick Hartwell's 'Grammar, Grammars, and the Teaching of Grammar' and the Composition of Anthology." *The Language Arts Journal of Michigan* 27.2 (Spring 2012): 57–62. Print.

Connors, Robert J., and Andrea A. Lunsford. "Frequency of Formal Errors in Current College Writing;, or Ma and Pa Kettle Do Research." *College Composition and Communication* 39.4 (December 1988): 395–409. Print.

Cureton, Richard D., et al. "Four Comments on 'Grammar, Grammars, and the Teaching of Grammar.'" *College English* 47.6 (October 1985): 643–45. Print.

Devet, Bonnie. "Welcoming Grammar Back into the College Classroom." *Teaching English In The Two-Year College* 38.1 (September 2002): 8–17. Print.

Elbow, Peter. *Writing Without Teachers.* New York: Oxford UP: 1973. Print.

Fulwiler, Toby. "How Well Does Writing Across the Curriculum Work?" *College English* 46.2 (February 1984): 113–25. Print.

—. "Showing, Not Telling, At a Writing Workshop." *College English* 43.1 (January 1981): 55–63. Print.

Hairston, Maxine. "Not All Errors Are Created Equal: Nonacademic Readers in the Professions Respond to Lapses in Usage." *College English* 43.8 (December 1981): 794–806. Print.

Hartwell, Patrick. "Grammar, Grammars, and the Teaching of Grammar." *College English* 47.2 (February 1985): 105–127. Print.

—. "Patrick Hartwell Responds." *College English* 47.6 (October 1985): 649–50. Print.

—. "Patrick Hartwell Responds." *College English* 47.8 (December 1985): 877–79. Print.

—. "Patrick Hartwell Responds." *College English* 48.4 (April 1986): 400–01. Print.

Huckin, Thomas. "A Comment on 'Grammar, Grammars, and the Teaching of Grammar.'" *College English* 48.4 (April 1986): 397–400. Print.

Hunter, Susan, and Ray Wallace. *The Place of Grammar in Writing Instruction: Past, Present, Future,* Portsmouth: Boynton/Cook, 1995. Print.

John of Salisbury. *The Metalogicon: A Twelfth Century Defense of the Verbal and Logical Arts of the Trivium.* Trans. Daniel D. McGarry. Berkeley: U of California P, 1962. Print.

Kolln, Martha. "A Comment on 'Grammar, Grammars, and the Teaching of Grammar.'" *College English* 47.8 (December 1985): 874–77. Print.

Lunsford, Andrea A., and Karen J. Lunsford. "'Mistakes Are a Fact of Life': A National Comparative Study." *College Composition and Communication* 59.4 (June 2008): 781–806. Print.

Micciche, Laura R. "Making a Case for Rhetorical Grammar." *College Composition and Communication* 55.4 (June 2004): 716–37. Print.

Moses, Carole, et al. "Four Comments on 'Grammar, Grammar, and the Teaching of Grammar.'" *College English* 47.6 (October 1985): 645–47. Print.

Noguchi, Rei. *Grammar and the Teaching of Writing: Limits and Possibilities.* Urbana: NCTE, 1991. Print.

Plato. *Gorgias.* Trans. by Benjamin Jowett. *The Internet Classics Archive.* Massachusetts Institute of Technology. Web. 10 Oct. 2013.

Sommers, Nancy. "Responding to Student Writing." *College Composition and Communication* 33.2 (May 1982): 148–56. Print.

Swilky, Jody. "Reconsidering Faculty Resistance to Writing Reform." *WPA: Writing Program Administration* 16.1–2 (Fall/Winter 1992): 50–61. Print.

Vavra, Edward A., et al. "Four Comments on 'Grammar, Grammar, and the Teaching of Grammar.'" *College English* 47.6 (October 1985): 647–49. Print.

Williams, Joe, et al. "Four Comments on 'Grammar, Grammars, and the Teaching of Grammar.'" *College English* 47.6 (October 1985): 641–43. Print.

Williams, Joseph M. Style: Ten Lessons in Clarity and Grace. New York: Longman. 2003. Print.

Appendix

Things _____ University Students Should Know About Writing

1. Use Commas Correctly

    A. Place a comma before coordinating conjunctions like "and," "but," "yet," "for," or "so" when these conjunctions separate two *full* sentences.

        The problem was significant, and many sought to solve it.
        We thought our hypothesis was correct, but the data showed otherwise.

    B. Set off introductory words, phrases (groups of words), and subordinate clauses with commas.

        Before Copernicus, the earth was thought to be the center of the universe.
        Today, we know the earth revolves around the sun.

    C. Set off an appositive (a re-statement of a noun that follows it directly) with commas *unless* it is necessary to define the noun that precedes it.

        Jane Austen, *the nineteenth-century novelist*, is still popular with readers.
        The nineteenth-century novelist *Jane Austen* is still popular with readers.
        For more, follow this link: https://owl.english.purdue.edu/owl/owlprint/607/

2. For Clear Sentences, Identify Actors and Their Actions

    As much as possible, make the verbs in your sentences actions, and actors the subject. Following this principle makes the (+) sentences below more clear.

        (–) The Wolf's words were, "Huffing and puffing will take place on my part, and your house will be blown in by me."
        (+) The Wolf said, "I'll huff, and I'll puff, and I'll blow your house in."
        (–) A study was undertaken in which the McGurk Effect at work in the human brain was examined.
        (+) Scientists studied the McGurk Effect at work in the human brain.

3. Semi–Colons Join Closely Related Sentences

        Use a semi-colon between two *full* sentences to show that the sentences are related in some way.

> The Federalists wrote in favor of the Constitution; the Anti-Federalists opposed them.
>
> Some doctors are concerned about the rising diagnosis rate of autism; they believe the condition should be redefined.

Read more on semi-colons here: https://owl.english.purdue.edu/owl/resource/607/04/

4. Use Colons To Add Emphasis and Introduce Lists That Are Appositives

A. Use a colon between two *full* sentences to emphasize the second sentence.

> –The Federalists had one goal: they wanted to persuade Americans to adopt the Constitution.

B. Colons also set up appositives:

> –The Federalists had one goal: to persuade Americans to adopt the Constitution.

C. Only use a colon before a list if the word immediately before the list is equivalent to the list itself.

> –We used the following materials: wooden dowels, eyehooks, rubber bands, and particleboard.
>
> Read more about colons here: https://owl.english.purdue.edu/engagement/2/1/44/

5. Identify and Fix Run-On Sentences

Run-on sentences are two or more full sentences that are not properly joined.

Fused sentences are joined with no punctuation at all.
> –We adjusted our design the car traveled the required distance.
>
> *Comma splices* join independent clauses with only a comma.
> –We adjusted our design, the car traveled the required distance.
>
> *A few common ways to fix run-on sentences:*
> Use a comma AND a coordinating conjunction.
> –We adjusted our design, and the car traveled the required distance.
> Use a subordinating conjunction.
> –Because we adjusted our design, the car traveled the required distance.
> Use a semi-colon to show a relationship between the sentences.
> We adjusted our design; the car traveled the required distance.

Read more on run-ons here: https://owl.english.purdue.edu/owl/resource/598/02/

6. *Identify and fix fragments*

Fragments are word groups that either lack a subject or verb, or they have an extra word that prevents them from standing as a sentence. Correct them by adding what's missing, or by joining them to another sentence. Examples below. (−) = fragments, (+) = corrected versions.

(−) The Supreme Court rulings known as "The Marshall Trilogy."
(+) The Supreme Court rulings known as "The Marshall Trilogy" played a key role in Indian dispossession.
(−) Since the data was inaccurate.
(+) Since the data was inaccurate, the conclusion is probably flawed.
(−) Suggesting that the conclusion may be flawed.
(+) They realized their data was imprecisely recorded, suggesting that their conclusions may be flawed.

Read more about fragments here: https://owl.english.purdue.edu/owl/resource/620/1/

7. *Prefer active voice, but use passive voice when it is appropriate, or standard practice*

Passive voice constructions always have a form of "to be" followed by a past participle verb:

PASSIVE: Conflicting policies were implemented.
ACTIVE: The Internal Revenue Service implemented conflicting policies.
(The active sentence here clarifies exactly who is implementing the policies.)

Writing in science and engineering sometimes uses passive voice when describing procedures. As a matter of style, passive voice is most often used to ensure a smooth flow or sequence of ideas. Passive voice is also appropriate when you wish to deemphasize the actor in favor of emphasizing the receiver or result of an action.

Read more on active and passive voice here: https://owl.english.purdue.edu/owl/resource/539/01/

8. *Fix Dangling and Disruptive Modifiers*

Make sure modifiers match up to the appropriate term. Here's a dangling modifier:

> –Claiming dozens of victims every day, doctors worked to contain the epidemic.

(This syntax suggests the doctors are claiming victims.)

To fix the problem, simply rephrase to reflect the logical connections:

> –Claiming dozens of victims a day, the epidemic posed a serious challenge for the doctors.

OR

> –The doctors worked to contain the epidemic, which claimed dozens of victims a day.

Here's a misplaced, or disruptive modifier:

> –Historians have debated whether Queen Elizabeth the First was a virgin for centuries.

To correct, simply straighten out the logic:

> –Historians have debated for centuries whether Queen Elizabeth the First was a virgin.

Read more here: https://owl.english.purdue.edu/engagement/2/1/36/

9. Ensure Clear Pronoun References/Antecedents

Make sure pronouns (like he, she, it, we, they, this, that, those) refer clearly to their antecedents.

> UNCLEAR: The two nations ignored their clean–air treaty, leading to many years of aggression, miscommunication, and environmental damage. This proved disastrous. (Exactly which part proved disastrous?)
> CLEARER: The two nations ignored their clean–air treaty, leading to many years of aggression, miscommunication, and environmental damage. *This refusal to comply with the provisions of the treaty* proved disastrous.

Read more here: https://owl.english.purdue.edu/owl/owlprint/595/

10. Craft Sentences that are Neither Choppy, Nor Rambling

Conjunctions can remedy both choppy writing (by combining sentences), and rambling sentences (by clarifying the relationships between ideas.)

Subordinating conjunctions (unless, until, as, as if, though, although, even though, when, that, than, before, after, while, since, because, so that) create subordinate clauses that both set up and give emphasis to the main clause.

–Although her argument was strong, I was not persuaded.

(Here, the idea of not being persuaded in the main part of the sentence is emphasized more than the idea in the subordinate clause of the argument being strong. Reversing the arrangement would reverse the effect.)

Coordinating conjunctions (for, and, nor, but, or, yet, so) give equal emphasis to two ideas, both of which could stand alone as a sentence:

–I agreed with her thesis, but I thought her evidence was weak.

(Here, the ideas of agreeing with the thesis and the weakness of the evidence are given equal emphasis by the co-ordinate conjunction "but.")

Note: In general, try not to have more than two or three clauses in a single sentence.

Read more here: https://owl.english.purdue.edu/engagement/2/1/37/

11. Follow a "Known–New" sequence in both syntax and paragraph development

To ensure a smooth prose style, make the opening words of each sentence tie into or refer back to the previous sentence, providing new information afterwards:

The Large Hadron Collider is an enormous machine that scientists use to study the universe. One important discovery the LHC brought about is the Higgs boson particle, which will help scientists understand why some particles have mass. The LHC may also help answer questions about the origins of the universe.

Here, the opening words in the second and third sentence link the sentence's idea to the first sentence. New information comes toward the end of each sentence.

Disciplining Grammar: A Response to Daniel Cole

JOANNA WOLFE

In "What if the Earth is Flat: Working With, Not Against, Faculty Concerns About Grammar in Student Writing," Daniel Cole relates the story of a faculty development workshop gone awry. A session on responding to student work—meant to introduce the commenting philosophies fundamental to writing studies—became derailed when faculty failed to accept the orthodoxy of deemphasizing grammar and sentence-level concerns in favor of global issues, such as content development, elaboration, and arrangement. As Cole notes, such conflicts between writing studies' principles and the beliefs of faculty in the disciplines are common.

Cole responds to the issue pragmatically, reasoning that we will ultimately have greater success in persuading disciplinary faculty of our writing across the curriculum/ writing in the disciplines (WAC/WID) philosophies if we make some effort to address what they see as the most pressing concerns with student writing. To this end, he provides a list created by faculty on his campus of ten "things" university students should know about writing—a list he hopes will be revised as needed, over the years, and accepted by all faculty at his institution. He ends with a call to bring "discussions of grammar pedagogy out of the margins, and reconsider how grammar instruction might be optimally reintegrated into our classrooms."

Cole should be commended for raising the issue of teaching grammar, which sometimes feels like a taboo subject in writing studies. As Cole notes—and as anyone who has extensively discussed writing with non-English faculty will confirm—writing studies' "orthodoxies" about addressing global problems before local ones often fail to persuade our colleagues from other disciplines. The importance of such persuasion is only growing as US colleges face increasing numbers of international students who do not speak English as their first language.

This response takes up Cole's call to better disseminate our field's understanding of grammar by sharing an activity, successful with faculty at Carnegie Mellon University, which helps disambiguate grammatical from other types of writing concerns. While Cole's list of common errors can help faculty prioritize certain writing issues and provide students with a consistent vocabulary across writing assignments, he acknowledges that his workshop attendees still "seem to assume that one who has learned grammar is a good writer." My activity is intended to confront this assumption.

Part of the problem is that individuals without any background in writing instruction tend to over-apply the term "grammar" (and even writing experts can disagree on what exactly this term includes). At its worst, such over-application can lead to radical misdiagnoses, akin to a driver with a flat tire peering under the engine hood to troubleshoot why the car is running so poorly.

As a case in point, in an unpublished study, my colleagues and I asked businesspeople to respond to emails containing a variety of errors. One email had many infelicities of tone and register, but contained no grammatical errors. Despite the fact that the email was error-free, fifteen percent of participants reported being bothered by its grammar, and one even cited "grammar" as the most problematic issue with the email. I have seen similar misdiagnoses play out in my communication center when faculty refer students to work on "grammar;" for example, when the student does not grasp the assignment or the readings they are responding to. Such misdiagnoses waste time and cause frustration as tutors struggle to explain to the student that fixing grammatical errors will still produce an essay that has missed the mark.

I share below an activity I have used to help disciplinary faculty confront beliefs about grammar. After asking faculty to compare the different versions of a one-paragraph text in Figure 1, I discuss my communication center's philosophy on grammar vis-à-vis other types of writing issues and describe the tools we have for addressing different types of writing problems. Consistently, well over eighty percent of participants in my workshops prefer version B. When I ask why, participants state that version B is easier to understand and that it "flows" better than the first version. Some may note that B moves from broad to specific—or as I frame it, version B invokes a clear macrostructure that enables readers to follow its logic.

I then ask participants if they noticed the grammatical errors in B. Heads nod. When I ask if they found the errors bothersome, participants volunteer that they were bothered but that they still found version B more comprehensible than A.

I then point out that while version B has over one grammatical error per sentence, version A has none. The two versions also have identical content. The differences that make participants prefer B lies entirely in organization and coherence.

Someone will inevitably point out that the ordering of the passages seems to stack the deck in favor of B (an observation I readily acknowledge) since content may be easier to comprehend on a second reading. A participant might also point out that the errors in B, while copious, are not particularly egregious: none interfere with our ability to understand the author's point, and none are sentence-boundary errors, which multiple studies have confirmed are particularly bothersome (Beason, 2001; Gilsdorf & Leonard, 2001; Hairston, 1981). More egregious errors might very well affect which passage participants prefer. In fact, the errors in B are typical of those we might expect from a non-native English speaker—missing articles, incorrect prepositions, wrong verb tense—which may make readers more sympathetic to the writer than had the errors been more typical of those made by native speakers.

Here are two versions of an introduction to a research project written for a general audience. Which do you prefer: A or B?

A. Polylactic acid (PLA) is a thermoplastic aliphatic polyester typically derived from corn starch, tapioca or sugarcane. Current uses for PLA include biodegradable medical implants, packing materials, diapers and 3D printers. We propose a device that composts PLA and other bioplastics within a home composting environment [1]. PLA and other bioplastics may provide a sustainable alternative to petroleum plastics, which have staggering environmental impacts. PLA resembles traditional plastic and can be processed on equipment already used for petroleum plastics. PLA biodegrades under carefully controlled conditions, but it is only compostable in industrial facilities and cannot be mixed with other recyclable materials [2, 3]. This makes the commercial viability of PLA limited. We argue that our device would encourage the production of more sustainable and economic bioplastics.

B. Although plastic has revolutionized modern life, the environmental impacts of traditional petroleum plastics is staggering. Bioplastics may provide sustainable alternative to petroleum plastics because it use fewer fossil fuels in production and reduce greenhouse gas emissions as they biodegrade. One particularly promising bioplastic are polylactic acids (PLA), a thermoplastic aliphatic polyester typically derived from corn starch, tapioca or sugarcane. PLA resembles traditional plastic and can be processed on equipment already used for petroleum plastics. However, the commercial viability for PLA is currently limited because is only compostable in industrial facilities and cannot be mixed with other recyclable materials [1, 2]. To make PLA more commercially viable, we propose a device that composts PLA and other bioplastics with home composting environment [3]. Such a device, we argue, would encourage production of more sustainable and economic bioplastics.

Figure 1. Exercise used in faculty writing workshops to explain our philosophy on grammar. Our communication center's tutors wrote both passages.

The exercise is intended to make a point, and it is one that most participants come to acknowledge: grammatically correct sentences are not the *sine qua non* of good writing. I then go on to present two fundamental tenants of my communication center's philosophy:

1. Readers are more forgiving of grammatical errors when the logic and organization are sound.

This is a rephrasing of writing studies' philosophy that global issues are more important to a text's readability than local ones. However, I think the nuances in phrasing are important. The above statement simply claims that when we improve organization, coherence, and logical development, grammatical errors appear less devastating than they might otherwise. In support of this point, I ask participants to imagine a passage combining the problems of version A and B and posit that some would identify the central textual problem of this imaginary text as one of grammar. However, these same readers are able to—if not overlook—at least provisionally absolve some of these errors when the logic, organization, and coherence of the passage are strong.

2. We have effective tools for teaching organization, coherence, and elaboration, but our tools for teaching grammar are much less effective; therefore, it is pragmatic to address the problems we are best positioned to improve

This point is central to arguments about why writing studies prioritizes "global" concerns over "local" ones. It is not just that we see "global" errors as more important—we can all think of essays where "local," grammatical errors overshadow a writer's attempts to communicate—but that we have better tools for addressing global errors. By tools, I mean concepts such as following a clear macrostructure, placing main arguments in topic sentences, or beginning sentences with given information and ending with new. I can effectively teach one or more of these concepts in a one-hour consultation and have a writer be at least partially successful in applying it in his or her next essay. My success rate is far lower for addressing grammatical error—particularly when working with non-native English speakers.

As a case in point, consider the exercise above. We can transform version A into version B by applying two organizational principles. The first is to follow the rhetorical conventions John Swales (1990) and others (c.f., Anthony, 1999; Samra, 2005) have identified as governing the introductions to research articles. Our well-organized version follows these conventions by beginning with a statement of significance, summarizing the status quo, identifying a gap, and then filling this gap with the researchers' own innovation. By contrast, version A fails to follow any predictable macrostructure. I am usually able to teach students the research introduction macrostructure in an hour or less. Students generally find the lesson persuasive and are able to grasp its principles relatively quickly.

The second principle we applied to transform version A into B is the given/new contract (often referred to as the known/new or old/new contract). This principle is based in the work of Michael Halliday (Halliday & Matthiessen, 2004) and was popularized for scientific writing by Gopen and Swan (1990). While slightly more difficult for writers to grasp and apply independently than the research introduction macrostructure, the given-new contract is typically easier to grasp than most grammatical rules.

In contrast to the two lessons needed to address the organization and coherence issues in version A, version B has at least six different types of errors. Further complicating matters is the fact that some of these errors are lexical rather than grammatical, meaning that they lack clear rules (Myers, 2004). For instance, I have no simple and compelling way of explaining why sentence five should read "the commercial viability *of* PLA" rather than "the commercial viability *for* PLA" or why an article is needed before "sustainable alternative" but not "greenhouse gasses" in sentence two. Such lexical knowledge, Meyers argues, can only be acquired through immersion in a language and may take years to develop. Even the subject/verb agreement errors in passage B (arguably the most teachable errors in the passage) are difficult to parse out since the passage contains so many complex noun phrases.

We need to admit to those outside of writing studies that our disciplinary tendency to address grammatical errors at a later stage in the writing process has as much to do with the intractable nature of grammatical problems as with the relative importance we place on this type of error. While some writing practitioners may object to the public acknowledgment that our tools are flawed, I think our disciplinary colleagues tend to understand. They all have research questions or problems in their disciplines that suffer because they are difficult or expensive to study. Our field has a similar situation with respect to grammar. The rules of English syntax and mechanics are notoriously complex, copious, and idiosyncratic. Enormous amounts of time are required to make small gains. By contrast, much less effort can yield large gains in organization, content development, and coherence.

Our colleagues in the disciplines need us to instruct them to distinguish different types of errors, and they need tools that can help them address such errors. Examples of such tools can be found in the handouts and videos at http://www.cmu.edu/gcc/HandoutsandResources/index.html. This site also contains resources discussing organizational patterns in scientific and technical disciplines as well as those common in the humanities. My communication center has had great success in sharing these tools with disciplinary faculty and departments.

Yes, we need to listen carefully and avoid assuming that we completely understand the rhetorical conventions of disciplines far afield of our own. This does not mean, however, that our faculty workshops should wait for good pedagogy and rhetorical understanding to emerge from our participants. We need to be prepared to provide concrete advice and tools that can help faculty recognize and teach the organizational macrostructures and rhetorical conventions common in their disciplines. At the same time, we also need to be flexible enough to modify or temper our advice when we discover disciplinary expectations that conflict with what we think we know.

My activity and discussion ultimately may not have persuaded the participants in Cole's workshop of the need to de-emphasize grammar, but it does provide a starting point. Along with providing lists such as Cole's, we need to teach our disciplinary colleagues how to diagnose and troubleshoot a range of textual problems.

References

Anthony, L. (1999). Writing research article introductions in software engineering: how accurate is a standard model? *IEEE Transactions on Professional Communication, 42*(1), 38-46.

Beason, L. (2001). Ethos and Error: How Business People React to Errors. *College Composition and Communication, 53*(1), 33-64.

Cole, D. (2014). What if the Earth is Flat: Working With, Not Against, Faculty Concerns About Grammar in Student Writing. *The WAC Journal,* 25. http://wac.colostate.edu/journal/

Gilsdorf, J., & Leonard, D. (2001). Big stuff, little stuff: A decennial measurement of executives' and academics' reactions to questionable usage elements. *The Journal of Business Communication, 38*(4), 439-475.

Gopen, G. D., & Swan, J. A. (1990). The science of scientific writing. *American Scientist, 78*(Nov-Dec), 550-558.

Hairston, M. (1981). Not all errors are created equal: Nonacademic readers in the professions respond to lapses in usage. *College English, 43*(8), 794-806.

Halliday, M. A. K., & Matthiessen, C. M. I. M. (2004). *Introduction to functional grammar* (3rd ed.). New York: Routledge.

Myers, S. (2004). Reassessing the "Proofreading Trap": ESL Tutoring and Writing Instruction. *Writing Center Journal, 24*(1), 51-70.

Samraj, B. (2005). An exploration of a genre set: Research article abstracts and introductions in two disciplines. *English for Specific Purposes, 24*(2), 141-156.

Swales, J. (1990). *Genre Analysis: English in Academic and Research Settings.* Cambridge: Cambridge University Press.

Knowing What We Know about Writing in the Disciplines: A New Approach to Teaching for Transfer in FYC

JOANNA WOLFE, BARRIE OLSON, AND LAURA WILDER

In recent years, composition studies has seen a considerable growth of interest in the transfer of learning, with researchers asking what abilities and knowledge students take with them from first-year composition (FYC) and use in new contexts. Anyone familiar with this line of inquiry will immediately be struck by how dismal the discoveries have been. Study after study, starting from Lucille P. McCarthy's 1987 research, has found that students fail to transfer writing knowledge from FYC to the writing they do in other coursework (Beaufort; Wardle, "Understanding"; Bergmann and Zepernick; Carroll). Worse, sometimes students negatively transfer knowledge, applying precepts learned in FYC to contexts where such advice is rhetorically inappropriate (Beaufort; Walvoord and McCarthy). The news is not all bad: two recent studies have reported positive results for students' abilities to transfer general rhetorical skills to later writing contexts (Brent; Johnson and Krase) and some teacher-researchers have proposed new curricula for FYC that they hope will encourage transfer (Downs & Wardle; Yancey, Robertson, and Taczak). However, absent these major curricular changes, most research suggests students see little occasion or need to transfer rhetorical knowledge from FYC to other disciplinary contexts.

Although some studies attribute such lack of transfer to students' dispositional characteristics (Driscoll and Wells; Reiff and Bawarshi), others fault the instructional approaches typical to FYC. For instance, Elizabeth Wardle states that "one reason for lack of transfer is instruction that does not encourage it" ("Mutt" 770), noting that composition instruction rarely encourages students to explicitly consider the connections between genres assigned in FYC and those of other disciplines. Similarly, Dana Driscoll observed composition instructors simply telling students they would use writing knowledge from FYC in future contexts but doing little to help them anticipate or build bridges to those future contexts.

One of the most prevalent reasons why FYC so often fails to promote transfer of learning is likely that writing instructors perceive their own academic writing experience as much more universal than it really is. As Wardle puts it, many FYC instructors mistake "the genres of English studies for genres-in-general" ("Mutt" 769). Consequently, these instructors see no need to prime students for the different genre work most will encounter. Such a generalized conception of writing is reinforced by the academic culture of specialization. Because instructors primarily teach and study within their disciplines, they come to mistake their specialized disciplinary ways of thinking and writing as universal skills (Russell, *Writing*; Lea and Street; Thaiss and Zawacki; Wilder). No more immune to this tendency, FYC instructors, frequently trained in literary studies (as recent collections edited by Anderson and Farris and by Bergmann and Baker make clear), tend to view their own discipline's values, assumptions, and conventions as the norms in other disciplines.

At their worst, such universalizing assumptions can result in giving students incorrect or harmful advice. For instance, Jo Mackiewicz observed writing center tutors, whose disciplinary background is often similar to FYC instructors, not only giving engineering students inappropriate advice that reflected the conventions of humanities writing but also stated inappropriate advice "with certainty" (316). Ghanashyam Sharma similarly encountered engineering faculty who felt their graduate students' visits to the university writing center actually made their writing worse. Joanna Wolfe found that technical writing textbooks typically written by English faculty, often give humanities-focused advice, such as uncritically promoting the active voice, or telling students that all documentation styles are similar to either MLA or APA ("How"). Heather Graves discovered the rhetorical moves advised by a popular, ostensibly trans-disciplinary textbook for graduate students were not evident in any of the scientific disciplines she examined.

More likely, however, this tendency to see the rhetoric of one's own discipline as universal simply leads instructors to downplay, or even deny, rhetorical differences among disciplines, even when they emerge before their eyes. For example, Rebecca Nowacek found that three faculty from literature, religious studies, and history team-teaching an interdisciplinary course had very different notions of what they meant by a thesis. However, when these differences appeared in classroom discussions, the faculty immediately suppressed them, encouraging students to see similarities that did not in fact exist. Laura Wilder's interviews of literature faculty indicate this phenomenon is not uncommon. For instance, one professor shared with students her belief that no fundamental differences exist between writing about literature and writing in other disciplines like psychology or biology, yet she recognized, and even welcomed, the different ways of thinking that diverse majors exhibited. Thus, "while she acknowledge[d] that different majors have different cultures . . . she resist[ed] seeing writing as one of the cultural practices in which these disciplinary differences may manifest" (Wilder 75). Driscoll similarly describes FYC instructors who claim their goal is to teach "general academic writing" or state "all majors go through a similar research process," but who also confess that they have no idea what engineers write or that "I don't know if scientists write papers; I kind of think not" (12-13). Such tendencies to gloss over rhetorical differences—or deny the presence of rhetoric in other disciplines—would seem to promote negative transfer of rhetorical knowledge if students follow their writing instructors' advice in contexts where that advice is inappropriate.

However the differences in rhetorical conventions and expectations that students encounter in different academic contexts have sometimes been emphasized to the extent that the possibility of transfer seems unlikely, if not impossible. For instance, Ken Hyland argues against general "academic literacy" instruction by claiming "each [disciplinary] discourse community has unique ways of identifying issues, asking questions, solving problems, addressing its literature, criticising [sic] colleagues and presenting arguments, and these make the possibility of transferable skills unlikely" (145). Similarly, David Russell, in an oft-cited passage, draws an analogy between writing in the academy and ball handling skills in sports to argue that "there is no autonomous, generalizable skill called ball using or ball handling that can be learned and then applied to all ball games" ("Activity" 57). While we agree with other WID researchers that different disciplinary discourse communities represent unique activity systems, we also see some commonalities across these systems. For instance, most academic writing, whether composed by students or their professors, is argumentative (Johnson and Krase; C. Wolfe) and addressed to an insider audience of disciplinary experts who will evaluate the work's merits. Most academic writing, regardless of discipline, also shows evidence that the writer has been disciplined and open-minded, privileging reason over emotion (Thaiss and Zawacki; Thonney), characteristics that again distinguish it from other discourses. In addition, academic writing announces its value (Thonney), often by claiming to present or create new knowledge (Kaufer and Geisler). As a consequence, proper attribution of others' work is much more significant in academic writing than in other discourses (Jameson; Thonney). In terms of Russell's analogy, the games played with words within the academy may require similar-enough "word handling" skills to make some transfer among academic games possible.

More importantly for our purposes, however, is that rhetorical skills need not be universal across all academic genres for transfer to occur across individual disciplines. Certainly, we should expect to find substantial overlap in the rhetorical conventions of closely related disciplines. Moreover, even epistemically diverse disciplines are likely to share *some* similarities. We believe that FYC instructors can do much more to prepare students to take advantage of these similarities—even while familiarizing themselves with the differences. However, first, instructors must educate themselves about how their own rhetorical knowledge may or may not transfer to other academic contexts.

Our own attempts to teach for rhetorical transfer borrow from research in two branches of English as a Foreign Language—English for Academic Purposes

(EAP) and English for Specific Purposes (ESP)—to flesh out an analytic method we term Comparative Genre Analysis (CGA) that can be integrated into a range of approaches to FYC. CGA involves careful comparison and contrast of the values and conventions of a genre one is already conversant in with those of other less familiar genres in order to better understand the larger activity systems in which both genres function. In an academic context, CGA can be used to better understand the core intellectual values that motivate writing in various disciplinary contexts. The assumption behind CGA is that by recognizing the particular rhetorical conventions of our discipline—*and* cultivating an awareness of how these conventions support disciplinary values and ways of knowing—we position ourselves to better understand the conventions and values laden in other disciplinary genres.

This essay combines an extensive review of relevant WID research with our own original analysis to perform a CGA that we hope will increase FYC instructors' awareness of academic writing outside of English studies. We accomplish this by comparing and contrasting the conventions of literary analysis with those of common genres in six other disciplines. We use literary analysis as a departure point because it is a relatively stable genre with which most new writing instructors are intimately familiar. Our goal is (1) to persuade FYC instructors that they are teaching specific rhetorical conventions rather than automatically generalizable writing skills and, more importantly, (2) to demonstrate how instructors can combine their discipline-specific expertise with an awareness of other academic contexts to help students intentionally transfer rhetorical knowledge already possessed.

We also propose CGA as a pedagogical strategy that is particularly useful for FYC sections intended to prepare students for academic writing. Some teacher-researchers, strongly influenced by recent research in genre, have already incorporated elements of CGA in their textbooks and pedagogical recommendations (Wardle and Downs; Devitt, Reiff, and Bawarshi). However, we would like to see such work integrated into a greater variety of FYC approaches, including expressivist, cultural studies, and argumentative approaches. The extensive CGA we perform in this essay not only gives instructors a rhetorical background that will bolster their confidence in discussing non-humanities academic writing, but also allows us to develop a framework of questions that can help students perform their own CGAs. We believe that conducting their own CGAs will heighten students' meta-awareness of rhetorical differences among academic genres—just as linked interdisciplinary courses or double-majoring improves students' abilities to recognize and articulate rhetorical differences among disciplines (Nowacek; Thaiss and Zawacki). Moreover, tasks such as CGA that ask students to explicitly link genre conventions to disciplinary values and goals can help students realize there is no universal criteria for "good writing" (Wilder 161-62).

We proceed by comparing and contrasting literary analysis with the conventions found in genres from six diverse disciplines: Business, Psychology, Nursing, Biology, Engineering, and History. We chose these disciplines for their diversity as well as their relative popularity among undergraduates (the first four fall under the academic areas that the National Center for Education Statistics cites as granting the most undergraduate degrees). In choosing so many fields we have obviously sacrificed thoroughness in favor of variety, but we do so because in this model CGA we are more interested in defining a set of questions that writing instructors can use to better prepare students to navigate the values and conventions of a range of academic disciplines. The disciplinary genres we consider include both pure academic genres, written for an audience of disciplinary experts, as well as pre-professional genres (common in disciplines such as Business) which may invoke external, non-academic audiences as well as the academic audience of the course instructor.

To narrow the scope of our investigation, we focus on three areas of rhetorical analysis that correspond to the three canons of invention, arrangement, and style:

- *Topoi*, or lines of argument, prevalent in a discipline.
- Macrostructures used to arrange arguments in the discipline.
- Naming and citation conventions used to refer to other scholars and their research.

For each discipline, we synthesized as much WID and EAP research as we could find touching on the above conventions. We supplemented this synthesis with discipline-specific textbooks and essays written by teachers and practitioners in those disciplines describing what they are looking for in student writing. Since naming of rhetorical conventions is inconsistent across this discourse, we had to extrapolate from the descriptions various researchers provided to our own framework. We then did our own primary research, examining undergraduate essays published in undergraduate research journals and conference collections and essays that individual instructors had posted to pedagogical websites as examples of model student papers. Our rationale in selecting these sources was that such essays would exemplify good, if sometimes advanced, undergraduate writing in these disciplines. We examined these essays for evidence of the rhetorical conventions described in the literature—or in cases where we could not find discussions of particular conventions, we conducted our own analysis based on our review of this undergraduate work.

Topoi

Special topoi, as Aristotle describes them, are mental "places" where the rhetorician goes to find the available means of persuasion in a particular context. These are a finer-grained version of what Michael Carter calls "ways of knowing" in a discipline

(387). However, where Carter's analysis allows him to group a range of academic assignments into a few meta-genres and meta-disciplines, our analysis identifies specific rhetorical activities that span such groups. This analysis allows us to foreground similarities across genres and disciplines with very different "ways of doing" (Carter 388). Consequently, our topoi embody values that Christopher Thaiss and Terry Myers Zawacki identify as universal to academic discourse: they emphasize reason over emotion and foreground disciplined inquiry that anticipates the response of a skeptical reader.

We begin our analysis by identifying the special topoi of literary analysis—a genre familiar to most FYC instructors. These topoi were originally identified by Jeanne Fahnestock and Marie Secor and Laura Wilder. Because the current analysis is interested in spanning disciplines, we abstract from this earlier work to articulate two topoi prominent in literary analysis that are evidenced in other disciplines. We call these *common academic topoi* because they are sufficiently common to span multiple academic disciplines yet still specialized enough that they may not be seen in the same permutations outside of academic discourse.

Pattern + Interpretation

The first common academic topos we consider, *pattern + interpretation*, is a combination of Fahnestock and Secor's special topoi of *appearance/reality* and *ubiquity*. Wilder found that these two topoi played prominent roles in nearly all of the published literary analyses she examined. Moreover, Laura Wilder and Joanna Wolfe note that these two topoi nearly always work together to support arguments in literary analysis, justifying our grouping of them here. An academic writer using the pattern + interpretation topos identifies a pattern in the primary material under analysis and uses this pattern to generate or support an interpretation. Figure 1 shows how pattern + interpretation works in an analysis of Milton's *Paradise Lost*. The underlined words in example 1 all show the writer pointing out a pattern of scientific imagery in the poem, finding evidence of this pattern in the serpent's words, Eve's actions, and the sensory nature of the Fruit itself. Tracing these patterns requires the writer to make a series of mini-definitions, interpreting various images, such as the sensory nature of the Fruit, as scientific imagery. Once the writer has made a compelling case for a pattern, he groups these mini-definitions under a larger interpretation about the significance of scientific imagery for the text as a whole.

> Not only does Milton frame Eve's actions in the language of <u>empirical science</u>, but he also
> _{pattern1}
>
> couches the <u>Fruit and the Tree of Knowledge in scientific imagery</u>. For instance, the Serpent
> _{pattern1}
>
> calls the Tree a "Sacred, Wise, and <u>Wisdom-giving Plant</u>" (IX. 679) and, strikingly, the
> _{pattern1}
>
> "<u>Mother of Science</u>" (IX. 680)… The combination of the Serpent's words, the lunchtime hour
> _{pattern1}
>
> of Noon, and the Fruit itself provoke each of Eve's five senses and increase her desire to eat
>
> from the Tree of Knowledge (IX. 736-42). <u>The Fruit, then, is metonymic for science, as both</u>
> _{pattern1}
>
> <u>appeal to sensory experience</u>….Both Eve and the Serpent conflate <u>wisdom with science and</u>
> _{pattern2}   _{pattern1 & 2}
>
> <u>experience</u>…**By closely associating science, experience, and sense perception with Satan**
> _{interpretation}
>
> **and the fall, Milton provides a sharp moral critique of this type of epistemology.**

Figure 1. Pattern + Interpretation in Literary Analysis (Ruby 82-83)

We found evidence of the pattern + interpretation topos in all six of the disciplines we examined. It is particularly common in situations that call for data- or text-driven discourse in which inquiry begins with primary material and uses disciplinarily appropriate methods to draw interpretations and conclusions about that material (MacDonald). Our review of research suggests students in various disciplines suffer common difficulties in implementing this topos. Just as literature students often write literary analyses that are heavy on plot summary and weak in interpretation, so do students in other disciplines often write essays that over-rely on description at the expense of interpretation. Thus, a history professor warns students "never regurgitate or summarize: look for the hidden truth or the unusual thread" (Writers' Web). Engineering mentors encourage novices to persuasively interpret data rather than simply provide data dumps of findings (Barabas; Winsor; Wolfe, Britt, and Alexander). Business instructors tell students to persuade readers by demonstrating patterns of evidence that align with their conclusion (Ellet). Psychology students are told to emphasize a "take home message" (Baumeister and Leary 316). In all of these cases, students must make rhetorical choices in describing patterns in datasets, research, or primary texts and use these descriptions to lead readers to particular interpretations or conclusions.

However, while the basic rhetorical moves of the pattern + interpretation topos appeared in all of the disciplines we reviewed, the following elements differed:

- the stasis—or the central issue at question—of the interpretation. Contemporary stasis theories typically define five main issues: existence, definition, evaluation, cause, and proposal
- the means of demonstrating the pattern—which can include observations, figures, tables, images, and statistical tests, as well as quotes and paraphrases
- the complexity of both the pattern and interpretation
- other topoi that may be combined with pattern + interpretation, most notably the topoi of *comparison* and *exception*.

A few examples should illustrate how this basic topos varies across disciplinary contexts.

Figure 2 shows how a business case analysis addresses different stasis issues and uses means that differ from those common in literary analysis. It begins with a clear argument in the topic sentence supported with evidence in the body—a method of arrangement familiar to those trained in literary analysis—but the evidence consists of observations rather than quotations. Moreover, where literary analysis makes arguments at the definitional stasis, this business case primarily operates at the evaluation stasis. This evaluation will assist the author in ending with a recommendation, reflecting business' emphasis on practical action. The lack of quotations, paraphrases, and documentation further illustrates business' concern with actions rather than texts and words.

The current organization cannot succeed because **it is misaligned, and Rogers has to take much**
interpretation
of the responsibility. He made organization changes that **ran counter to the division's past and**
restating interpretation
were not guided by a clear vision. New product development has suffered because Rogers made
pattern
changes....He moved the division headquarters to corporate...Sales and marketing were
pattern   *pattern*
separated with no consideration for their complementary nature....The marketing people can't
pattern
collaborate effectively with sales...yet he is not coaching and helping them
pattern

Figure 2. Pattern + Interpretation in Business Case Study (Ellet 111).

Whereas Figure 1 shows how a pattern develops by interpreting texts and Figure 2 by evaluating actions, Figure 3 shows how a pattern develops by interpreting and comparing numbers:

> This study resulted in a conclusion that <u>only 5.3% of athletes wearing the newer helmet</u> [*pattern1: fewer concussions*] <u>suffered a concussion</u> <u>compared to</u> [*comparison*] <u>7.3% of athletes wearing the older models</u>.... Overall, high school players <u>wearing Riddell's Revolution were 31%</u> [*pattern1: fewer concussions*] <u>less likely</u> [*comparison*] <u>to be diagnosed with a concussion.</u> <u>Table (1) shows that out of athletes sustaining their first concussion,</u> [*pattern2: shorter down time*] <u>those wearing the Revolution were able to return to game</u> <u>sooner than</u> [*comparison*] those who were wearing standard head gear. **The Revolution Helmet protects the player** [*interpretation*] **better than** [*comparison*] **standard helmets.**

Figure 3. Pattern + Interpretation in Engineering Experimental Report (Gonzales and Matthews 3-4).

Figure 3 uses percentages, tables, and text to identify two closely related patterns that support the interpretation that the new helmets offer better protection than the standard. These patterns are established through the common academic topos of *comparison*—one of the most common rhetorical moves in scientific discourse (Fahnestock; Walsh). Our analysis of primary texts found the comparison topos combined with *pattern + interpretation* in quantitative arguments in a variety of disciplines, suggesting that *comparison* is a major means for constructing knowledge out of numerical data.

Although those trained in literary analysis may be tempted to dismiss the numbers in Figure 3 as arhetorical facts, the percentages and other numbers included represent rhetorical decisions about how to present data involving dozens of unique incidents (J. Wolfe, "Rhetorical Numbers"). The authors had many choices for displaying the data; they selected representations that guide readers to conclude the new helmet is better. Because engineering students often shy away from clearly stating such conclusions based upon their data—perhaps out of a fear of being found wrong in high-stakes situations, or perhaps out of a belief that numbers can speak for themselves (Winsor; J. Wolfe, "How"; Wolfe, Britt, and Alexander)—there appears to be a real need for instruction in argumentation for these students.

Figure 4 shows a final mutation of the *pattern + interpretation* topoisin a biology lab report. This example uses text, percentages, a figure, and statistical tests to demonstrate a pattern: germination increases as GA_3 increases. However, the interpretation of this pattern does not appear until the discussion section, several paragraphs later, when the writer explicitly states what has been learned about GA_3. This convention of defining patterns in the results section and waiting until the discussion to state what they mean helps promote a scientific stance of neutrality (Graves; Stockton, "Students") that focuses attention on observable phenomena rather than interpretative acts (Bazerman). Thus, some disciplines foreground patterns while others, like literary analysis, foreground interpretations.

The example in Figure 4 additionally makes use of the *exception* topos, a common—and often challenging—rhetorical move in scientific and technical disciplines where writers need to explain aberrant or unexpected results, couch negatives as positives, or concede weaknesses in methods (Herrington; Walsh; J. Wolfe, "How"). Students, unsurprisingly, struggle with how and when to acknowledge exceptions without detracting from their main arguments (Herrington; Walker). In fact, the writer of Figure 4 ultimately dedicates as much text to exceptions as to the primary argument. Instructors experienced in reconciling conflicting readings of texts can help students make similar arguments reconciling conflicting interpretations of quantitative data.

In the light, germination success of seeds of the *gal-3* mutant increased from 6% to
                    pattern1   *comparison*

97.8% with increases in GA_3 concentration from 0 to 0.5 mol L^{-1} (Fig. 1). A similar trend with
                                                        pattern1   *pattern1*

increasing GA_3 concentration was observed in seeds maintained in darkness.

A two-way analysis of variance (Table 1) showed that the effect of GA_3 concentration
                                                                                       pattern1

on germination success was highly significant ($P < 0.001$). However, there was no significant
                                                                                     Exception

difference ($p > 0.05$) in germination success between seeds kept in the light and those kept in
                                                                                            comparison

the darkness.

Figure 4. Pattern + Interpretation in Biology Lab Report. The interpretation appears several paragraphs later, in the discussion section (McMillan 98).

Finally, writing instructors should be critically attuned to the role *pattern + interpretation* plays in literature reviews—a commonly assigned genre in Business, Psychology, Nursing, and Biology (Johnson and Krase) and one we find both students and novice writing instructors frequently misunderstand. For instance, in one writing center session we observed, a student explicitly described her organizational plan for a sociology literature review as discussing one source per page. This plan went unchallenged by the two tutors she visited on different days. In contrast to this atomized approach, nearly every source we examined about literature reviews stressed the need to avoid simple summary and instead use the literature review to argue for connections, or patterns, in the research and make interpretations. Thus, Roy F. Baumeister and Mark R. Leary state that psychology literature reviews should not "merely recount" previous research, but instead fulfill the "broader imperative" of explaining "how the various studies fit together" (317). Teresa Smallbone and Sarah Quinton describe business literature reviews as "reconstruct[ing] material into a new pattern" (7). Helen Aveyard advises nursing students to make a chart of key themes so that they can "begin to see patterns emerging in the literature." Victoria E. McMillian urges Biology students to articulate "relationships, patterns, and arguments" in the literature (115). The message is clear: literature reviews use the *pattern + interpretation* topos to articulate patterns in the research that the writer interprets in a "nuanced conclusion" (Anglim) which often points to the need for additional research.

Conceptual Lens

Our second major common academic topos, the conceptual lens, uses a concept—a term, theory, or hypothesis—to organize observations about the phenomenon under study. In literary analysis, *conceptual lens* involves using a theory as a lens for analyzing primary texts (Fahnestock and Secor refer to this topos as a *paradigm*). Anyone who has used Bakhtin's concept of heteroglossia, DuBois' double-consciousness, or Lacan's gaze to analyze a text has engaged this topos. Conceptual lens involves, at a minimum, two distinct rhetorical moves: (1) present the concept and then (2) apply this concept to interpret primary material. We see these two moves at work in Figure 5.

Foucault distinguishes the Panopticon from the prisons of history in that, unlike a traditional
present/ summarize concept

dungeon…the Panopticon turns an intense spotlight on each individual within its cells….

[In *Villette*,] **Madame Beck believes constant, methodical surveillance** to be her
apply concept

best recourse in maintaining control over her school, which becomes a microcosm of

Bronte's Victorian context **as teachers, students, and headmistress act out Bentham's**
apply concept

description of the Panopticon.

Figure 5. Conceptual lens in literary analysis (Bertonneau 21-22).

The writer in Figure 5 first summarizes Foucault's panopticon and then applies this theory at the definitional stasis to interpret the characters in Bronte's novel.

Sophisticated uses of the conceptual lens topos go on to include a third move: using the analysis itself as an occasion for redefining or reflecting on the original concept. Such redefinition is often missing from student discourse: in some cases, instructors do not require it while, in others, students are unsure of how to do it—or simply unaware that such reinterpretation is even expected. Figure 5 gestures towards this final move later in the essay by explaining how the protagonist manages to "beat the Panopticon" (24) and "def[y] the Foucaultian prison of categorization by defying understanding" (29). In this way, individual works of literary criticism may refine and revise literary theory (Wilder 38).

The example in Figure 6 uses similar rhetorical moves to fulfill the nursing goal of reflecting on (and consequently improving) practice. Although the stasis is definition, the example in Figure 6 makes no attempt to redefine the theories or concepts; instead, the writer uses *conceptual lens* to prepare herself for future practice.

Severtseen (1990) cited by Duxbury (2000) applies the term therapeutic communication as the *present/ summarize concept* dialogue between nurse and patient to achieve goals tailored exclusively to the patient's needs. In this case **dialogue is used by Mr. Comer in the form of body language and noise to** *apply concept* **communicate his needs because of speech loss.**

Figure 6. Conceptual Lens in Nursing Reflective Essay (Pure Maiden)

The conceptual lens topos also appears in hypothesis-driven research, where it serves the disciplinary goal of testing and extending knowledge. In such contexts, the conceptual lens topos serves the evaluation stasis by testing the merits of the hypothesis. In Figure 7, a psychology student tests whether theoretical insights on racial stereotypes can be applied to the domain of regional stereotypes and concludes that the hypothesis can be supported.

This study hypothesizes that Southern accented speakers will be perceived as more friendly, less Wealthy, more aggressive, and less intelligent than Standard accented speakers.... Overall, these hypotheses take the theoretical approach of many race-based stereotype studies that suggest *present/ summarize concept* socially salient cues activate stereotypes, leading to perceptual shifts. In cases of regional stereotyping, accent alone may trigger such powerful social perceptions. *extend concept with analogy*

Figure 7. Conceptual Lens in Psychology (Phillips 54)

We found evidence of the conceptual lens topos in all of the disciplines we surveyed, with the exception of Biology (an exception that could reflect the limits of our literature review rather than rhetorical practice in Biology). The ultimate ends to which this topos was put varied across disciplines, but we found evidence of students struggling to match data—whether from texts, personal experience, or study results—to pre-existing concepts in their work with most of the disciplinary genres we examined. The chief difficulty students seemed to encounter with this topos lay in trying to use vocabulary and concepts they did not fully understand (Abasi and Akbari). Such appropriation can lead to patch-writing as students attempt to reproduce ideas they do not fully grasp (Howard). A second common problem occurs when students assume an assignment is asking them to display their understanding of the *conceptual lens* rather than transform or apply this understanding. FYC instructors can prepare students to apply the conceptual lenses they encounter in other disciplines by naming this strategy when it occurs in our own assignments (see Appendix A) or class readings and illustrating how discipline-specific concepts and vocabulary help writers make sense of phenomena—whether that phenomena be texts, data, observations, or personal experiences.

Macrostructures

Whereas our analysis of topoi stresses similarities between literary analysis and other disciplines, our discussion of macrostructures points to some dramatic differences. A macrostructure is a top-level organizational pattern that provides informed readers with a frame of reference that helps them make sense of the text (D'Angelo). This frame of reference helps informed readers recall important information and reduces reading time.

The primary macrostructure in literary analysis is the thesis-first argument. This structure has two primary functions: it summarizes the main argument(s) of the paper and it forecasts the paper's organizational structure. Thesis-first argument is so pervasive in English studies and much of the Humanities that many composition instructors may be guilty of believing an early and clear thesis statement is the *only* way to organize an argument effectively.

Unfortunately, the thesis-first argument is not necessarily the standard in other disciplines. Heather Graves explains that learning this argumentative style has "helped countless undergraduate students learn to write effective arguments for their first year writing and liberal studies classes" (1). Unfortunately, Graves goes on to explain, "once students leave composition and liberal studies classes […], these methods of argumentation may not be as useful in helping them argue effectively in the discourse of their chosen majors" (1). Even within the liberal arts, the thesis-first argument is not necessarily standard (see Table 1).

Table 1. Most Common Genres and Macrostructures in the disciplines we discuss.[2]

Discipline	Common Genres	Primary Macrostructure
Literature	Literary analysis	Thesis-first
Business	Case study Proposal	Problem solution Problem solution
Psychology	Experimental report Literature review	IMRD Thesis-first
Nursing	Reflection/Care report	Chronological
Biology	Lab report Literature review	IMRD Thesis-last
Engineering	Design paper Experimental report	Problem-solution IMRD
History	Historical analysis[3]	Thesis-first or thesis-last

Note: IMRD refers to Introduction-Method-Results-Discussion

Table 1 shows thesis-first was the dominant macrostructure in only three of the major disciplinary genres we examined in addition to literature. This is not to say that thesis-first essays were absent from other disciplines, but they were not the primary macrostructure organizing the most common genres in these disciplines. It is also important to note, however, that many of the genres (including nursing reflections and biology literature reviews) did contain a statement of purpose in a position FYC instructors might associate with the thesis, but the primary propositions in the essay did not appear in this position.

Many readers will perhaps be surprised by the prominent role that thesis-last macrostructures play in historical analysis, a genre similar in many ways to literary analysis. Anne Beaufort claims that whether historians explicitly state a central argument and where they place it seems to be at the writer's discretion (71), an analysis supported by Caroline Coffin. When we asked one history colleague who told us she wanted students to include an explicit thesis at the beginning of the paper what she thought of the thesis-last structure, she quickly told us "that is valid too." Sharon Stockton describes how many historians embed implicit arguments into a "narrative structure" (56) rather than state them explicitly, offering conclusions only after demonstrating they have carefully considered all of the evidence. When students use the explicit argumentative structures favored in literary analysis in their history papers, many professors perceived their writing as "unsophisticated" and "too forceful" (Stockton, "Writing" 63).

Thesis-first argument predominates in literary analysis because it enables readers to follow complex and highly nuanced arguments. Although historians clearly also value complex and sophisticated arguments, they may often privilege ethos and narrative sophistication over logical signposting. For instance, one historian advocating a thesis-last macrostructure told his students "You don't set out to prove something; you set out to see where the evidence leads you" (Nowacek 106). Similarly, natural scientists often favor thesis-last writing in literature reviews because it projects a scientific ethos of humility (Bazerman) in which scientists as interpreters are subordinated to the natural phenomena they document. Graves explains how the thesis-last argument projects an ethos of neutrality: not only does the focus remain on results rather than interpretation but scientists use implicit argument to allow discussion of others' research to remain "essentially descriptive, neutral, and objective" (13).

While the thesis-last macrostructure allows scientists to emphasize their neutrality, the IMRD (Introduction-Methods-Results-Discussion) macrostructure common in many science and social science disciplines emphasizes the communal ethos of fields characterized by rapid knowledge dissemination and accumulation. In contrast to the individualistic nature of thesis-driven arguments, which often need to be read from start to finish to be fully comprehended, IMRD reports are written to allow readers to find specific information quickly. Carol Berkenkotter and Thomas Huckin describe how scientists read for newsworthiness, engaging in "a scanning and reading pattern dominated by the search for interesting new information" (30). The IMRD structure facilitates such searching by foregrounding the most important information in multiple sections: typically the abstract, title, and beginning of the discussion section. Some sections, such as the methods section, are typically read by a minority of readers who often are searching for specific information that will help them validate the credibility of the methods. More information on the IMRD structure can be found at http://www.cmu.edu/gcc/handouts/IMRD.pdf. While writers accustomed to the linear unfolding of thesis-driven arguments may feel that IMRD reports are repetitive and stifle creativity, there are also similarities between the two macrostructures in that both require writers to foreground new and important arguments in predictable places.

Problem-solution macrostructures are most common in applied disciplines, such as Business and Engineering (Ellet; C. Wolfe), and support these disciplines' values of efficiency (Eustace; Louhiala-Salminen) by creating a structure that is flexible and easy to skim. Problem-solution essays typically rely on document design to highlight main propositions and signal the argumentative structure. The example in Figure 8 shows how a business case study uses headings and parallelism (both visual and grammatical) to allow readers to quickly scan main ideas without becoming bogged down in details.

3.1 Solutions for Motivating the WPC Employees
3.1.1 Appoint a WPC employee to two solicitors
Each data clerk should be appointed to two solicitors where possible. This would allow the WPC emp WPC employee's work area could be near the office of their designated solicitor. All data clerks on the perform a greater number of activities instead of doing the same thing all day. Consequently, this woul greater initiative, establishing responsibility and loyalty. It would also provide better training for becomi every week to discuss problems and issues. However, WPC employee skills may not improve becaus to discipline the girls and prevent them from arriving late, talking and slacking off. They may not be abl improve.
3.1.2 Have different levels of data clerks
This would create a work environment where the girls would be willing to work harder in order to receiv undisciplined work behaviour. It would provide better efficiency and create fewer errors because in ord their tasks correctly. It would also identify where the errors are occurring. The clerks on the highest lev

Figure 8. Problem/Solution macrostructure in business case study (CALT Learning)

Although problem-solution and IMRD essays look very different from thesis-first arguments, all three macrostructures provide similar functions in that they foreground the most important information readers will need in fairly predictable places: near the end of the introduction, in the abstract, in the headings. FYC instructors can therefore explain how similar principles of arrangement function in these diverse macrostructures while avoiding the misconception that thesis-first organization is universal.

Naming and Citation

Stylistic differences between genres, such as differences among citation conventions, tend to be among the most noticeable. In this section we examine how disciplinary values and scholarship practices inform stylistic conventions such as how and when to cite, whether to use direct quotation, and how explicitly to foreground other authors.

Table 2 illustrates the citation differences among three different disciplines: literature, psychology, and electrical engineering. While the use of the same sources across citation formats in Table 2 may promote the misconception that citation style is a purely technical matter unrelated to content (Dowdey 346), the use of the same sources allows us to highlight key differences that reveal disciplinary assumptions about research and authorship. We often provide such an example to students and ask them to reflect on the differences among these styles and what they mean for the various disciplines. Students immediately point to the prominent date in the APA style, which reflects the importance of recent knowledge in the social sciences, and IEEE's (Institute of Electrical and Electronics Engineers) use of numbers rather than author names, which reflects the high value this discipline places on concision and the comparatively low value it places on individual authorship.

Table 2. Citation styles across three disciplines. The first two rows illustrate in-text citations while the last illustrates the works cited.

MLA	APA	IEEE
Snyder calls the concept "medium-fidelity prototyping" (35).	Snyder (1999) calls the concept "medium-fidelity prototyping" (p. 35).	The concept has been called "medium-fidelity prototyping" [5].
Many educators agree that students suffer from insufficient unstructured play time (Anderson; Capps, Stevens, and Brown; Smith, Taylor and Johns)	Many educators agree that students suffer from insufficient unstructured play time (Anderson 1999; Capps, Stevens, and Brown 2004; Smith 2000; Taylor and Johns 2008)	Many educators agree that students suffer from insufficient unstructured play time [6-9].
Honneycutt, Lee. "Comparing Email and Synchronous Conferencing in Online Peer Response." Written Communication 18.1 (2001): 26-60. Print. Margolis, Jane, and Allan Fisher. Unlocking the Clubhouse: Women in Computing. Cambridge, MA: MIT Press, 2002. Print.	Honneycutt, L. (2001). Comparing email and synchronous conferencing in online peer response. Written Communication, 18(1), 26-60. Margolis, J., & Fisher, A. (2002). Unlocking the clubhouse: Women in computing. Cambridge, MA: MIT Press.	[2] L. Honneycutt, "Comparing email and synchronous conferencing in online peer response," Written Communication, vol. 18, pp. 26-60, 2001. 1] J. Margolis and A. Fisher, Unlocking the Clubhouse: Women in Computing. Cambridge, MA: MIT Press, 2002.

Overall, these various conventions reflect differences in what Susan Peck MacDonald calls compact and diffuse disciplines. Compact disciplines, where large numbers of scholars focus on a small number of relatively well-defined problems, are characterized by co-authorship, large numbers of recent citations, and low importance placed on individual authorship. Such disciplines tend to have citation conventions that facilitate multiple citations and deemphasize author names. By contrast, diffuse disciplines, with a large range of loosely defined problems and relatively few scholars working on each one, are characterized by individual authorship and fewer current citations. Their citation conventions reflect this individuality and particularity.

Diffuse and compact disciplines also differ in how they handle controversy. In diffuse disciplines, knowledge is more particular, scholars are more likely to refer to one another by name, and disagreement is more pointed. For instance, Robert Madigan, Susan Johnson, and Patricia Linton quote an author in literary studies referring to a critic as "truculently persist[ing] in crediting the discredited" and another describing an alternative view as "willful revisionism" (431). Laura Wilder similarly observes critics directly naming and disagreeing with others in statements such as, "In this light, [X]'s argument….requires amendment" (43). Wilder goes so far as to describe such rhetorical moves as a special topos in literary studies—one she tellingly names "mistaken critic" (42).

By contrast, although controversies occur in compact disciplines, writers tend to avoid naming individuals and instead focus on knowledge claims. Madigan, Johnson, and Linton claim confrontational disagreements are rare in psychology and are explicitly discouraged by the APA publication manual (431). Roy F. Baumeister and Mark R. Leary elaborate:

> Good writing of literature reviews [in psychology] requires a concerted effort to feature the findings and ideas. Downplaying the names of researchers (such as by putting citations in parentheses) is a valuable stylistic device for ensuring that the article focuses on ideas and research rather than on theorists and researchers. It also helps the writer to avoid the appearance of making *ad hominem* arguments. (320)

Greg Myers, likewise, states that biologists rarely cite other authors to refute claims, but instead to show parallels or alternative explanations.

The extent to which different disciplines privilege individuality and particularity of knowledge extends to their attitudes towards direct quotation. MLA style contains copious rules for citing different types of texts and managing quotations of varying lengths and direct quotations are common. Such frequent quotation may reflect a belief that meaning is inseparable from its expression (Madigan, Johnson, and Linton); or it may simply indicate that literary analysis is concerned with text and textual matter—an emphasis it shares with history, which also has a high rate of direct quotation (Madigan, Johnson, and Linton 430). By contrast, IEEE style lacks a mechanism for citing page numbers, illustrating how rare direct quotations are in scientific and technical disciplines. In fact, Victoria E. McMillan explicitly warns Biology students against direct quotation, which she claims suggests the writer "is either too inexperienced or too lazy to use his or her own words" (124). Direct quotations are also rare in psychology, causing problems for students who have been taught by composition instructors to quote the exact language of their sources (Madigan, Johnson, and Linton 433).

Even stylistic conventions such as voice can be linked to disciplinary values. For instance, Joanna Wolfe ("How") has argued that the preference for passive voice in engineering reflects this discipline's tendency to privilege things rather than people whereas scholars in the humanities prefer active voice because it places grammatical focus on individual actors and texts. Following similar logic, nursing tends to privilege active voice and direct quotation (Dexter) because of its focus on individual human agents while biology uses passive voice to downplay the role of human agency and focus attention on nature (Stockton, "Students"; Bazerman). Thus, stylistic conventions that may at first seem arbitrary are linked to larger disciplinary values (see Soliday for a more thorough discussion). Students need to be attuned to these values because genres that have the same name may have different conventions depending on the discipline. A nursing student will be rewarded for using direct quotation and active voice in a literature review while a similar style will be perceived as laziness or lack of mastery in a biology literature review. FYC instructors should help prepare students to look for the rationale and values underlying such preferences—rather than perceive them as bewildering arbitrary expectations.

Conclusion

Our CGA presents a large amount of information about genre differences in a small space. Our analysis is limited both by our choice to start with literary analysis as a point of departure (which causes us to miss topoi central to other disciplines but peripheral in English) and by the limited space we have to discuss important rhetorical issues such as stance (Hyland; Soliday), ways of doing (Carter), or stasis. We have shown commonalities in rhetorical topoi across very different disciplines and academic tasks. At the same time, our CGA also shows how different our discipline's arrangement and stylistic preferences can be from other academic writing students will perform. These differences are major enough that—without explicit coaching—many students will be unable to look past them to see the similarities. Such concern is lent support by Linda S. Bergmann and Janet Zepernick's finding that students dismissed much of their training in composition as irrelevant to the writing they do in other disciplines. Matthew Wiles likewise found disciplinary faculty reinforcing this mindset by explicitly telling students to forget what they learned about writing in FYC.

We hope that many FYC instructors will find our analysis provocative and this provocation will encourage them to provide more scaffolding to help students apply rhetorical knowledge from FYC to future academic (and pre-professional) writing tasks. Much as Liane Robertson, Kara Taczak, and Kathleen Blake Yancey have argued that students need to understand that they lack critical knowledge to be motivated to take up rhetorical challenges they have not previously understood, we hope that our CGA will point to lacunae and blind spots in FYC instructors' rhetorical knowledge that will motivate them to seek out other similarities and differences in the writing assigned in their institutional context.

But what should FYC instructors do with the knowledge that we hope our CGA will foster? We want to clarify first that we are *not* proposing that FYC instructors attempt to master the conventions of other disciplines. Such mastery is unrealistic, and in any case, it would be nearly impossible to decide which disciplines' conventions to teach. Instead, we propose that FYC instructors develop some meta-awareness of recurring differences and commonalities between their own rhetorical knowledge and that manifested in other disciplines and attempt to impart some of that meta-awareness to their students.

In particular, we propose that FYC instructors look for ways—both large and small—to integrate elements of CGA into their curriculum. CGA can teach students to extract genre features from model texts and learn what questions to ask in new rhetorical environments—skills that Doug Brent associates with successful transfer. If students can learn to tie the rhetorical similarities and differences they observe to the values underlying particular academic discourse communities, we believe they will be develop a "flexible" rhetorical knowledge that will prepare them to *transform* rather than simply *transfer* rhetorical principles across contexts (Brent 565).

Thus, we offer a multi-tiered proposal suggesting a variety of ways instructors can incorporate elements of CGA into their classes:

1. At the most basic level, FYC instructors can call attention to the common academic topoi used in their assignments and connect these topoi to other contexts students are likely to encounter in future academic work. Appendices A and B provide examples of how instructors might label the common academic topoi and macrostructures used in a literacy narrative and evaluation argument, respectively. These handouts both conclude with discussions of how these topoi function in other fields and how the skills practiced in a thesis-first macrostructure will prepare students to prioritize and arrange information in other organizational structures. Such labeling and contextualization helps students develop meta-knowledge about rhetorical strategies that lays the groundwork for rhetorical transfer.

2. We also encourage FYC instructors to explicitly discuss one or two academic readings that do not use a thesis-first macrostructure. In particular, we recommend examining the IMRD macrostructure since, without explicit discussion, the differences between IMRD and the thesis-driven essay will likely overwhelm students' abilities to see any commonalities. A concise summary of the IMRD macrostructure can be found at http://www.cmu.edu/gcc/handouts/IMRD.pdf. We encourage instructors to spend part of a class period discussing how IMRD constrains writers' freedom, but allows readers to skim and read non-sequentially. Students can be asked to brainstorm about how the macrostructures and stylistic differences typically found in IMRD reports vs. thesis-first essays reflect the values of the scholarly communities where these formats are typically found.

   One good way to choose an IMRD text is to select a research study cited in a reading already on the course syllabus. For instance, we have had success pairing sections from Levitt and Dubner's *Freakonomics* with Levitt's academic articles discussing his research. Such pairing not only allows students to analyze differences in style and arrangement in academic and popular texts, but also provides them with opportunities to compare topoi across popular and academic texts. For example, where Levitt's academic articles use *conceptual lenses* from economics such as *profit maximization* and *cannibalization*, such lenses are absent from his popular texts. Both texts use *pattern+interpretation*, but only in the academic article does the reader see the data: readers of the popular text must trust the author's conclusions with minimal evidence.

In short, we are recommending that instructors include some readings that look very different from those typical in FYC and they use class discussion to lead students through a mini-CGA. Appendix C contains a list of questions that can be used to guide such CGAs.

3. Finally, we also recommend including CGA as a class assignment or class unit, a practice already found in some genre-based textbooks, such as Amy J. Devitt, Mary Jo Reiff, and Anis Bawarshi's *Scenes of Writing* (463, 465). Appendix D presents an extended example of one such assignment. Students are asked to pick a topic of interest and compare and contrast how this topic is presented in academic journals from two different disciplines and a popular magazine, newspaper, or blog. Students then use their observations to make recommendations about what writers need to keep in mind when writing for the audiences of these different publications. Such assignments introduce students to the process of library research, but do not require that students fully comprehend this research—comprehension that may be beyond their, and our, abilities. Instead, students use the results of their library research as a form of data out of which they can make arguments.

Assigning a CGA addresses one problem in our analysis here: namely that we anchor our discussion in literary analysis, looking at how topoi and stylistic conventions common in this discipline manifest themselves in other academic discourse communities. Students who start their own CGAs with a different discipline will likely turn up other topoi and conventions. Thus, by assigning CGA, instructors will increase their knowledge of other academic discourses—knowledge that they can then use to develop even more connections between FYC and other academic writing contexts. Unlike many recent curricular proposals for FYC, instructors can implement elements of CGA without overhauling their current curriculum. However, we also want to stress that the benefits of CGA would likely stretch further if integrated into a Writing about Writing program or a pedagogy such as Yancey, Robertson, and Taczak's Teaching for Transfer (TFT) in which students work to develop a "theory of writing" that will provide them with a framework for assignments they take with them elsewhere (57). We also hope that the CGA we have presented in this essay will provide instructors who do take up these pedagogical programs with more information about the types of transfer they may want to promote.

We would like to end by discussing the important role we believe CGA should play in instructor training if any of the above recommendations are to be implemented in the FYC classroom. While we are aware that the teaching practicum required of many new instructors already covers too much, we argue that significant attention to CGA is a worthy addition—even in programs where FYC is intended less as preparation for academic writing than for personal expression or civic participation. At the very least, including CGA in the practicum can reduce instructors' tendencies to perpetuate misleading and inaccurate writing instruction. Likewise, we believe some exposure to CGA is essential to the preparation of writing center tutors. Writing centers have long wrestled with the thorny problem of employing tutors who lack expertise in the rhetorical practices of the disciplines they aim to support writers to work in (Shamoon and Burns; Walker). CGA should not only discourage tutors from mistaking the conventions of familiar disciplines as universal norms, but can also give them specific criteria to look for when encountering unfamiliar genres.

In sum, we believe FYC needs more attention to genre, and that instructors in particular need more exposure to unfamiliar genres both inside and outside of the humanities. FYC will be a better preparation for students' future academic writing if instructors have a clearer idea of the types of rhetorical challenges their students will face. CGA is one method for helping both students and instructors take a clearer stock of their existing rhetorical knowledge and its potential future applications.

Notes

1. Rhetoricians typically subordinate topoi to stasis, making the stasis the larger lens under which various topoi fall. Our analysis reverses this hierarchy, allowing us to see commonalities in topoi that might otherwise be obscured.

2. This table draws on the following sources: *Literature:* Wilder and Wolfe; *Business:* Ellet; Forman and Rymer; C. Wolfe; Zhu; *Psychology:* Baumeister and Leary; Baron; Johnson and Krase; Madigan, Johnson, and Linton; Mitchell, Jolley, and O'Shea; *Nursing:* Craft; Gimenez; Jasper; Johnson and Krase; *Biology:* Graves; Haas; Johnson and Krase; McMillan; *Engineering:* Carter; Johnson and Krase; C. Wolfe; J. Wolfe, "How"; Wolfe, Britt and Alexander; *History:* Beaufort; Coffin; Nowacek; Stockton.

3. Although several researchers have proposed classifications for various historical genres (c.f., Beaufort; Coffin), these classifications would likely be unfamiliar to many historians.

Works Cited

Abasi, Ali R, and Akbari, Nahal. "Are We Encouraging Patchwriting? Reconsidering the Role of the Pedagogical Context in ESL Student Writers' Transgressive Intertextuality." *English for Specific Purposes* 27 (2008): 267-84. Print.

Anderson, Judith H., and Christine R. Farris, eds. *Integrating Literature and Writing Instruction: First-Year English, Humanities Core Courses, Seminars.* New York: MLA, 2007. Print.

Anglim, Jeromy. "How to Write a Literature Review in Psychology." *Jeromy Anglim's Blog: Psychology and Statistics.* Ed. Anglim, Jeromy: Blogspot, 2009. Web. 24 June 2012.

Aveyard, Helen. "Top Tips for Doing Your Literature Review!" *Nursing Times.net.* Web. 15 July 2012.

Barabas, Christine P. *Technical Writing in a Corporate Culture: A Study of the Nature of Information.* Norwood: Ablex, 1990. Print.

Baron, Jonathan. "How to Write a Research Report in Psychology." *Upenn.edu*, 1991. Web. 8 Aug. 2012.

Barton, Ellen L., Matthew Aldridge, and Robert Brown. "Personal Statements: A Conversation with John Swales and Chris Freak." *Issues in Writing* 15.1 (2004): 5-30. Print.

Baumeister, Roy F., and Mark R. Leary. "Writing Narrative Literature Reviews." *Review of General Psychology* 1.3 (1997): 311-20. Print.

Bawarshi, Anis. *Genre and the Invention of the Writer: Reconsidering the Place of Invention in Composition.* Logan: Utah State UP, 2003. Print.

Bazerman, Charles. "What Written Knowledge Does: 3 Examples of Academic Discourse." *Landmark Essays in Writing across the Curriculum.* Ed. Charles Bazerman and David R. Russell. Florence: Routledge, 1994. 159-88. Print.

Beaufort, Anne. *College Writing and Beyond: A New Framework for University Writing Instruction.* Logan: Utah State UP, 2007. Print.

Bergmann, Linda S., and Edith M. Baker, eds. *Composition and/or Literature: The Ends of Education.* Urbana: NCTE, 2006. Print.

Bergmann, Linda S., and Janet Zepernick. "Disciplinarity and Transfer: Students' Perceptions of Learning to Write." *Writing Program Administration* 31.1-2 (2007): 124-49. Print.

Berkenkotter, Carol, and Thomas N. Huckin. *Genre Knowledge in Disciplinary Communication: Cognition, Culture, Power.* Hillsdale: Erlbaum, 1995. Print.

Bertonneau, Marie. "'La vie d'une femme': Surveillance and Subversion in Charlotte Brontë's *Villette*." *Criterion: A Journal of Literary Criticism* 5 (2012): 19-30. Web. 15 July 2012.

Brent, Doug. "Crossing Boundaries: Co-Op Students Relearning to Write." *College Composition and Communication* 63.4 (2012): 558-92. Print.

CALT Learning Support. "Amy's Sample Assignment." *Language and Learning Online.* Monash University. 21 Feb 2007. Web. 20 Sep 2013.

Carroll, Lee Ann. *Rehearsing New Roles: How College Students Develop as Writers*. Carbondale: Southern Illinois UP, 2002. Print.

Carter, Michael. "Ways of Knowing, Doing, and Writing in the Disciplines." *College Composition and Communication* 58.3 (2007): 385-418. Print.

Coffin, Caroline. "Learning to Write History: The Role of Causality." *Written Communication* 21.3 (2004): 261-89. Print.

Craft, Melissa "Reflective Writing and Nursing Education." *Journal of Nursing Education* 44.2 (2005): 53-7. Print.

D'Angelo, Frank. "The Topic Sentence Revisited." *College Composition and Communication* 37.4 (1986): 431-39. Print.

Devitt, Amy J. *Writing Genres*. Carbondale: Southern Illinois UP, 2004. Print.

Devitt, Amy, Mary Jo Reiff, and Anis Bawarshi. *Scenes of Writing*. New York: Pearson, 2004. Print.

Dexter, Phyllis. "Tips for Scholarly Writing in Nursing." *Journal of Professional Nursing*, 16.1 (2000): 6-12. Print.

Dowdey, Diane. "Citation and Documentation Across the Curriculum." *Rhetorical Education*. Eds. Marie Secor and Davida Charney. Carbondale: Southern Illinois UP, 1992. 330-52. Print.

Downs, Douglas, and Elizabeth Wardle. "Teaching About Writing, Righting Misconceptions: (Re)Envisioning 'First Year Composition' as 'Introduction to Writing Studies.'" *College Composition and Communication* 58.4 (2007): 552-84. Print.

Driscoll, Dana. "Connected and Disconnected Pedagogy and Transfer of Learning: An Examination of Instructor Beliefs Vs. Practices in First-Year Writing." 2012. Print. Unpublished ms.

Driscoll, Dana, and Jennifer H. M. Wells. "Why Individuals Matter: Writing Transfer and the Role of Student Dispositions In and Beyond the Writing Classroom." 2012. Print. Unpublished ms.

Ellet, William. *The Case Study Handbook: How to Read, Discuss, and Write Persuasively About Cases*. Boston: Harvard Business Review P, 2007. Print.

Eustace, Grant. "Business Writing – Some Aspects of Current Practice." *Engligh for Specific Purposes* 15.1 (1996): 53-6. Print.

Fahnestock, Jeanne. *Rhetorical Figures in Science*. New York: Oxford UP, 1999. Print.

Fahnestock, Jeanne, and Marie Secor. "The Rhetoric of Literary Criticism." *Textual Dynamics of the Professions: Historical and Contemporary Studies of Writing in Professional Communities*. Eds. Charles Bazerman and James Paradis. Madison: U of Wisconsin P, 1991. 76-96. Print.

Forman, Janis, and Jone Rymer. "Defining the Genre of the 'Case Write-Up.'" *The Journal of Business Communication* 36.2 (1999): 103-33.

Gimenez, Julio. (2008). "Beyond the Academic Essay: Discipline-Specific Writing in Nursing and Midwifery." *Journal of English for Academic Purposes* 7.3 (2008): 151-64. Print.

Gonzales, Juan M, and Ryan Matthews. "The Head Impact Telemetry System." Web. 4 Dec. 2012.

Graves, Heather. "Toward a Taxonomy of Argument in Dissertations and Theses in Science." 2012. Print. Unpublished ms.

Haas, Christina. "Learning to Read Biology." *Written Communication* 11.1 (1994): 43-84. Print.

Herrington, Anne J. "Writing in Academic Settings: A Study of the Contexts for Writing in Two College Chemical Engineering Courses." *Research in the Teaching of English* 19.4 (1985): 331-61. Print.

Howard, Rebecca Moore. "A Plagiarism Pentimento." *Journal of Teaching Writing* 11.2 (1992): 233-246. Print.

Hyland, Ken. *Disciplinary Discourses: Social Interactions in Academic Writing*. Harlow: Longman, 2000. Print.

Jameson, Daphne. "The Ethics of Plagiarism: How Genre Effects Writers' Use of Source Materials." *The Bulletin* June (1993): 18-28. Print.

Jasper, Melanie A. "Using Reflective Writing Within Research." *Journal of Research in Nursing* 10.3 (2005): 247-60. Print.

Johnson, J. Paul, and Ethan Krase. "Articulating Claims and Presenting Evidence: A Study of Twelve Student Writers, from First-Year Composition to Writing across the Curriculum." *WAC Journal* (in press). Web.

Kaufer, David S., and Cheryl Geisler. "Novelty in Academic Writing." *Written Communication* 6.3 (1989): 286-311. Print.

Lea, Mary R., and Brian V. Street. "Student Writing in Higher Education: An Academic Literacies Approach." *Studies in Higher Education* 23.2 (1998): 157. Print.

Louhiala-Salminen, Leena. "The Business Communication Classroom vs. Reality: What Should We Teach Today?" *English for Specific Purposes* 15.1 (1996): 35-51. Print.

MacDonald, Susan Peck. "Data-Driven and Conceptually Driven Academic Discourse." *Written Communication* 6.4 (1989): 411-35. Print.

Mackiewicz, Jo. "The Effects of Tutor Expertise in Engineering Writing: A Linguistic Analysis of Writing Tutors' Comments." *IEEE Transactions on Professional Communication* 47.4 (2004): 316-28. Print.

Madigan, Robert, Susan Johnson, and Patricia Linton. "The Language of Psychology: APA Style as Epistemology." *American Psychologist* 60.6 (1995): 428-36. Print.

McCarthy, Lucille Parkinson. "A Stranger in Strange Lands: A College Student Writing Across the Curriculum." *Research in the Teaching of English* 21.3 (1987): 233-65. Print.

McMillan, Victoria E. *Writing Papers in the Biological Sciences*. 5th ed. Boston: Bedford/St. Martins, 2012. Print.

Mitchell, Mark L., Janine M. Jolley, and Robert O' Shea. *Writing for Psychology*. Belmont: Wadsworth, 2010. Print.

Myers, Greg. "The Social Construction of Two Biologists' Proposals." *Written Communication* 2.3 (1985): 219-245. Print.

Nowacek, Rebecca. *Agents of Integration: Understanding Transfer as a Rhetorical Act.* Carbondale: Southern Illinois UP, 2011. Print.

Phillips, Taylor. "Put Your Money Where Your Mouth Is: The Effects of Southern vs. Standard English Perceptions of Speakers." *Stanford Undergraduate Research Journal* 9 (2010): 53-7. Web. 12 December 2012.

Pure Maiden. "Topic: 1st Year Reflective Essay Using Gibbs." *Nurserve.* Web. 4 Dec. 2012.

Reiff, Mary Jo, and Anis Bawarshi. "Tracing Discursive Resources: How Students Use Prior Genre Knowledge to Negotiate New Writing Contexts in First-Year Composition." *Written Communication* 28 (2011): 312-37. Print.

Robertson, Liane, Kara Taczak, and Kathleen Blake Yancey. "Notes toward A Theory of Prior Knowledge and Its Role in College Composers' Transfer of Knowledge and Practice." *Composition Forum* 26 (2012). Web. 20 August 2013.

Ruby, Ryan. "Reclaiming *Paradise Lost*: The Angelic Bias in Fish's Milton." *The Columbia Journal of Literary Criticism* 1 (2003): 79-90. Web. 15 July 2012.

Russell, David R. "Activity Theory and Its Implications for Writing Instruction." *Reconceiving Writing, Rethinking Writing Instruction.* Ed. Joseph Petraglia. Mahwah: Lawrence Erlbaum, 1995. 51-77. Print.

—. *Writing in the Academic Disciplines, 1870-1990: A Curricular History.* Carbondale and Edwardsville: Southern Illinois UP, 1991. Print.

Shamoon, Linda, and Deborah H. Burns. "A Critique of Pure Tutoring." *The Writing Center Journal* 15.2 (1995): 134-51. Print.

Sharma, Ghanashyam. "Ideological Tensions, Pedagogical Gaps: Multilingual Engineering Scholars' Response to Language Variation in Academic Writing." Diss. University of Louisville, 2012. Print.

Smallbone, Teresa, and Sarah Quinton. "A Three-Stage Framework for Teaching Literature Reviews: A New Approach." *The International Journal of Management Education* 9.4 (2011): 1-11. Print.

Smart, Graham, and Nicole Brown. "Learning Transfer or Transforming Learning? Student Interns Reinventing Expert Writing Practices in the Workplace." *Technostyle* 18.1 (2002): 117-41. Web. 26 July 2012.

Soliday, Mary. *Everyday Genres: Writing Assignments across the Disciplines.* Carbondale: Southern Illinois UP, 2011. Print.

Stockton, Sharon. "Students and Professionals Writing Biology: Disciplinary Work and Apprentice Storytellers." *Language and Learning Across the Disciplines* 1.2 (1994): 79-104. Print.

—. "Writing in History: Narrating the Subject of Time." *Written Communication* 12.1 (1995): 47-73. Print.

Swales, John M. *Genre Analysis: English in Academic and Research Settings.* Cambridge: Cambridge UP, 1990. Print.

Thaiss, Christopher, and Terry Myers Zawacki. *Engaged Writers Dynamic Disciplines: Research on the Academic Writing Life*. Portsmouth: Boyton/Cook Heinemann, 2006. Print.

Thonney, Teresa. "Teaching the Conventions of Academic Discourse." *Teaching English in the Two-year College* 38.4 (2011): 347-62. Print.

Walker, Kristin. "The Debate over Generalist and Specialist Tutors: Genre Theory's Contribution." *The Writing Center Journal* 18.2 (1998): 27-45. Print.

Walsh, Lynda. "The Common Topoi of Stem Discourse: An Apologia and Methodological Proposal, with Pilot Survey." *Written Communication* 27.1 (2010): 120-56. Print.

Walvoord, Barbara E., and Lucille Parkinson McCarthy. *Thinking and Writing in College: A Naturalistic Study of Students in Four Disciplines*. Urbana: NCTE, 1990. Print.

Wardle, Elizabeth. "'Mutt Genres' and the Goal of FYC: Can We Help Students Write the Genres of the University?" *College Composition and Communication* 60.4 (2009): 765-89. Print.

—. "Understanding 'Transfer' from FYC: Preliminary Results of a Longitudinal Study." *Writing Program Administration* 31.2 (2007): 65-85. Print.

Wardle, Elizabeth, and Douglas Downs. *Writing about Writing: A College Reader*. Boston: Bedford/St. Martin's, 2011. Print.

Wilder, Laura. *Rhetorical Strategies and Genre Conventions in Literary Studies: Teaching and Writing in the Disciplines*. Carbondale: Southern Illinois UP, 2012. Print.

Wilder, Laura, and Joanna Wolfe. "Sharing the Tacit Rhetorical Knowledge of the Literary Scholar: The Effects of Making Disciplinary Conventions Explicit in Undergraduate Writing about Literature Courses." *Research in the Teaching of English* 44.2 (2009): 170-209. Print.

Wiles, Matthew. *Prompting Discussion: Writing prompts, Habits of Mind, and the Shape of the Writing Classroom*. Diss. University of Louisville, 2013. Print.

Winsor, Dorothy A. *Writing Like an Engineer: A Rhetorical Education*. Mahway: Lawrence Erlbaum, 1996. Print.

Wolfe, Christopher R. "Argumentation across the Curriculum." *Written Communication* 28 (2011): 193-219. Print.

Wolfe, Joanna. "How Technical Communication Textbooks Fail Engineering Students." *Technical Communication Quarterly* 18.4 (2009): 351-75. Print.

—. "Rhetorical Numbers: A Case for Quantitative Writing in the Composition Classroom." *College Composition and Communication* 61.3 (2010): 434-57. Print.

Yancey, Kathleen Blake, Liane Robertson, and Kara Taczak. *Writing across Contexts: Transfer, Composition, and Sites of Writing*. Logan: Utah State UP, forthcoming. Print.

Wolfe, Joanna, Cynthia Britt, and Kara Alexander. "Teaching the IMRaD Genre: Sentence-Combining and Pattern Practice Revisited." *Journal of Business and Technical Communication* 25.2 (2011): 119-58. Print.

Writers' Web. "Principles of Historical Writing: Thinking Like an Historian." *University of Richmond Writing Center*. 2010. Web. 16 July 2010.

Zhu, Wei. "Writing in Business Courses: An Analysis of Assignment Types, their Characteristics, and Required Skills." *English for Specific Purposes* 23.2 (2004): 111-35. Print.

Appendix A: Assignment Foregrounding Conceptual Lens

Literacy Narrative

Overview

Deborah Brandt argues that literacy sponsors "set the terms for access to literacy and wield powerful incentives for compliance and loyalty. Sponsors are a tangible reminder that literacy learning though out history has always required permission, sanction, assistance, coercion, or, at minimum, contact with existing trade routes" (166-167). To that end, write a literacy narrative that describes the literacy sponsorship you received that ultimately led you to a seat in this classroom. In other words, reflect on the writer you are today and the role that literacy sponsorship (positive or negative) played in creating that writer. Be sure to reference the literacy sponsorship scholarship we've read as you write your narrative.

Goals

This assignment is designed to give you practice

- applying concepts you have learned about in class to your own experiences (this is a strategy we call using a **conceptual lens**)
- organizing information in a thesis-driven argument
- using detailed description as evidence supporting an argument
- developing appropriate tone, voice, and level of formality for academic writing

Evaluation Criteria

Criteria	Goal
Analysis	The essay clearly defines what literacy sponsorship entails, using relevant quotes and paraphrases from the course readings. The concept of literary sponsorship is then used to analyze details from the author's life to show how the literacy sponsorship influenced the author's literacy practices and development.
Organization	The essay uses a thesis-driven structure that places main arguments in the thesis and topic sentences. Each individual paragraph emphasizes one unique main idea that is clearly connected to the thesis statement. Paragraphs are arranged according to a logical principle and connected to one another with coherent transitions.
Mechanics & Style	The essay demonstrates appropriate word choices, a formal tone, and grammatically correct sentences.

How this assignment will help you with other academic writing

This essay asks you to take a concept discussed in course readings—literacy sponsorship—and apply it to personal evidence from your own life. We call this process using **conceptual lens** because you are using a concept developed by other scholars to interpret a particular set of information or data (in this case, your own life). Assignments asking you to apply a conceptual lens are particularly common in the social sciences and humanities where students are asked to use concepts such as *social distance, conflict theory,* or *paternalism* to interpret texts, documents, historical or cultural phenomena, or personal observations. We also find conceptual lenses in applied disciplines, such as nursing and business, where students are asked to apply concepts such as *therapeutic communication* or *diversification* to particular workplace practices.

This essay also asks you to follow a **thesis-driven** (or thesis-first) organizational structure. Practicing a thesis-first organization prepares you for other organizational structures by teaching you to prioritize your main claims by placing them in key locations (in this case, the thesis statement, topic sentences) that attract the reader's attention and provide a framework for understanding the details that follow.

Works Cited

Brandt, Deborah. "Sponsors of Literacy." *College Composition and Communication* 49.2 (1998): 165-85. Print.

Appendix B: Assignment Foregrounding Pattern + Interpretation

Entering a Conversation

Overview

In your academic writing, you will often be asked to synthesize and respond to the research and writings of other scholars in order to insert your own voice into a conversation. For instance, researched essays respond to what others have said or argued about an issue. Scientific studies begin with a review of other experiments on a topic. Business proposals survey current practices or approaches to a problem. Reviews of research studies (often called literature reviews) synthesize and evaluate a large number of studies on a topic.

This assignment asks you to practice the work of synthesizing and responding to others' writing in order to stake out your own position. However, instead of analyzing difficult texts on an academic topic, you will instead work with criticism from popular culture. This allows you to practice academic writing without the burden of also working to understand difficult academic subjects.

The Details

Pick a cultural artifact (a movie, TV show, video game or musical album) that is no more than two years old and has received mixed reviews from critics. Write a 3-5 page argument that identifies patterns, or trends, in the reviews and evaluates them using your own analysis of the cultural artifact. Your argument must fairly and respectfully respond to exceptions to your argument and interpretations that differ from your own.

Your argument must:

- include a short summary of the artifact you are defending
- paraphrase or quote at least three sources with which you disagree
- paraphrase or quote at least two sources with which you agree

Goals

This assignment is designed to give you practice

- **identifying patterns** (or trends) in the sources you cite (for instance, you may note that a majority of reviews criticize a particular actor or note "plot holes" in a film);
- **identifying patterns** in the artifacts you analyze (for instance, you may note a pattern of strong special effects in a video game or a pattern of "body humor" in a show);

- **interpreting** these patterns to support or reject an overall evaluation of your artifact;
- responding to **exceptions,** both to the patterns you identify and the interpretations you make;
- writing a **thesis-driven** argument; and
- paraphrasing and quoting from other authors as you insert your voice into ongoing arguments.

Evaluation Criteria:

Criteria	Goal
Analysis	The essay argues for patterns in the reviews you cite and in the artifact you analyze. The essay interprets these patterns in order to support or reject particular evaluations of your artifact.
Exceptions	Exceptions to the author's main arguments (or counter-arguments) are considered with respect and either conceded to or countered with logical arguments.
Organization	The essay uses a thesis-driven structure that places main arguments in the thesis and topic sentences. Each individual paragraph emphasizes one unique main idea that is clearly connected to the thesis statement. Paragraphs are arranged according to a logical principle and connected to one another with coherent transitions.
Mechanics & Style	The essay demonstrates appropriate word choices, a formal tone, grammatically correct sentences, and a correctly formatted list of works cited.

How this assignment will help you with other academic writing

This essay asks you to define patterns in the work you read and analyze and interpret these patterns for a particular purpose. We call this strategy **pattern+interpretation.** In this assignment, you are arguing for patterns in *texts*; in other academic writing, you may be arguing for patterns in *data, observations* or *practices*. However, regardless of *what* you are analyzing, the basic pattern+ interpretation strategy remains consistent. In a nutshell, it consists of

1. identifying a pattern
2. providing evidence to support that pattern and
3. interpreting that pattern to make or support an argument

This essay asks you to identify patterns across multiple texts. This is in many ways similar to a common assignment in the social sciences and sciences called a *literature review*. A literature review asks you to identify patterns in research methodologies or results across multiple research studies.

Another major component of this essay involves handling **exceptions** (or counter-arguments) to your argument. All academic disciplines require writers to acknowledge and respond to exceptions to their arguments. It is a particularly common—and challenging—part of research writing in science and engineering, where writers need to explain unexpected results, concede weakness in methods, or reconcile conflicting interpretations of quantitative data.

As with other assignments this semester, this essay requires a **thesis-driven** (or thesis-first) organizational structure that gives you practice situating your main claims in places that readers are most likely to focus on.

Appendix C: Analyzing Unfamiliar Academic Genres

TOPOI*

Definitions

Pattern + Interpretation

A writer using the pattern + interpretation topos identifies a pattern (such as a recurring theme) in the primary material under analysis and uses this pattern to generate or support an interpretation.

Conceptual Lens

The conceptual lens topos uses a concept—a term, theory, or hypothesis—to organize observations about the phenomenon under study.

Comparison

The comparison topos is used to illustrate the relationship between or among the items being studied or analyzed. It can often, though not always, be identified by the use of comparative adjectives or adverbs (as in, "simpler," "faster," "larger").

Exception

The exception topos is used to explain aberrant or unexpected results, couch negatives as positives, concede weaknesses in methods, or to acknowledge other anomalies in the analysis.

Questions

1. Does the text make substantial use of **pattern + interpretation**?
    - Is the pattern found in a text; across multiple texts; in numbers, figures, or data; in observations or workplace practices; in something else?
    - What interpretation is drawn from this pattern?
2. Does the text make substantial use of **conceptual lens**?

- What concepts are being used?
- What phenomena is the lens used to analyze? Is it analyzing texts, data, observations, practices?
- Does the writer attempt to redefine the conceptual lens?
3. Does the text make substantial use of **comparison**?
   - What is being compared? Is the comparison based on numbers, data, words, observations?
   - What interpretation or recommendation is being drawn from this comparison?
4. Does the text make substantial use of **exceptions?**
   - Where do these exceptions appear?
   - How does the author respond to these exceptions without detracting too much from the main analysis s/he wants to make?
5. What **stasis**—or type of question—is each topos being used to answer? Does it allow the writer to show that something exists (such as a new planet or species), define what something means, evaluate something, argue for causes and effects, or propose a solution to a problem?
6. How **complex** is the argument made with each topos? Is the argument fairly straightforward? Or does it require substantial explanation and interpretation?
7. What type of **values** do these topoi suggest? Do they emphasize logical reasoning? Fair-mindedness? Disciplined inquiry? Skepticism?

Macrostructure

Definitions

Thesis-first

A statement (or thesis) summarizing the main arguments of the essay and previewing the essay structure appears near the beginning of the essay.

Thesis-last

A thesis summarizing the main claim of the essay appears in the conclusion, after the writer has presented the evidence and demonstrated that they have done the research and analysis necessary to make this claim.

IMRD

Stands for Introduction-Method-Results-Discussion. This is a highly structured genre typical of experimental research (including lab reports) in which "newsworthy" information appears in the abstract, results, and discussion section and often the title.

Problem/Solution

The essay is divided into two somewhat parallel—although not equally weighted—sections: the problem and the solution section.

Questions

1. What **type of macrostructure** does this essay use?

2. Where is the **newsworthy** information found? In a thesis statement? In the title? The abstract? The conclusion? The headings? The figures or illustrations?

3. What does this organization suggest about the **values** of the community who will be reading it? Do they privilege quick reading? Logical progression of ideas? Establishing credibility?

Style & Citation

1. What **citation system** is used and what **disciplinary values** does it support? Does it privilege authors? Are ideas or information more important than who said them? To what extent does it privilege current research? Does it privilege conciseness and efficiency?

2. To what extent is **direct quotation** used in discussing other research?

3. How explicit is **disagreement**?

4. What types of **phrases** do authors use to align themselves with others' ideas? How do they express agreement or disagreement?

1. To what extent is **active voice** used?

* This handout focuses on topoi you are most likely to encounter in your writing classes. However, these are not the only topoi, and you may find others that are common to your field. Some additional topoi you may encounter include *generating solutions* (common in applied disciplines such as business or nursing where writers brainstorm solutions to a problem on paper), *justification of criteria* (used to justify selection criteria for experimental populations or articles to examine reviews of research), *argument by analogy* (where an extended comparison is made in order to explain a concept—such as the use of the "hand" metaphor in economics, used to discuss the invisible hand of the market).

Appendix D: Sample CGA Assignment

How Context Shapes Controversy: A Researched Comparison/Contrast Argument

Overview

As you take classes in disciplines across the university—and as you eventually move from the university to the workplace—you will continually be asked to adapt your writing style and methods. This essay prepares you for these shifts in your writing practices by teaching you to closely examine different genres, reading them in order to determine what features and rhetorical strategies you should mimic.

For this assignment, pick a controversial topic related to your future career and compare/contrast how this topic has been discussed in three different rhetorical contexts. For instance, you might look at recent research on a drug trial or dieting regime, the funding of public art, the role of nurse practitioners in medicine, or the environmental impact of electrical cars. You should then use your analysis to make recommendations for writing persuasively in each of these contexts.

The Details

Your essay should be 5-8 pages and do the following:
- Begin by introducing the topic and explaining why it is controversial
- Analyze multiple examples of writing from three different contexts including
    - peer-reviewed journals from two different disciplines
    - a popular source, such as a newspaper, blog, or popular magazine.
- Use both textual and numeric evidence to support your arguments
- Use your analysis to recommend effective writing practices in each of these contexts.
- Include a works cited page
- Organize the essay in either a thesis-driven or IMRD format.

Goals

In addition to teaching you how to read a text to select features that you can use as a model, this assignment is designed to give you practice

- **identifying patterns** *within* a particular genre or context and **interpreting** these patterns to show what they reveal about this community's values and practices (use the handout on "how to analyze an unfamiliar academic genre" to guide your analysis)
- **comparing and contrasting** these patterns *across* genres or contexts

- using these comparisons to **make recommendations** for writing practices
- **locating and citing** information from a wide variety of sources.
- **organizing** information in the form of a recognizable academic macrostructure

Evaluation Criteria

Criteria	Goal
Analysis	The essay argues for patterns *within* each different context and makes comparisons/contrasts *across* contexts. Patterns are interpreted in terms of what they reveal about rhetorical values and practices. Comparisons/contrasts are interpreted to make recommendations for how to adjust your writing practices in different contexts. Arguments are supported by both numerical and textual evidence.
Organization	The essay either has a clear thesis statement or clearly follows all parts of the IMRD genre. Each paragraph has a clear topic sentence and focuses on one main idea. Headings and subheadings are used effectively. Appropriate coherence strategies connect main ideas.
Mechanics & Style	The essay demonstrates appropriate word choices, a formal tone, grammatically correct sentences, and a correctly formatted list of works cited.

How this assignment will help you with other academic writing

As with other writing tasks this semester, this essay asks you to define patterns in the types of topoi and stylistic conventions in various writing contexts. You will then interpret these patterns to make arguments about the types of readers and writers who participate in these contexts. This basic strategy of ***pattern+interpretation*** is found in many academic contexts and can be used to interpret patterns in *data, numbers, observations*, and *practices* as well as texts.

This essay also asks you to compare/contrast the patterns you define across different contexts. **Compare/contrast** is a major academic strategy that is common when we want to compare the merits of two items or factors or to compare groups to understand what makes them unique. In this essay, you will use compare/contrast to define what makes different writing situations unique. This is similar to how social scientists might compare/contrast different cultural groups, educators different types of learners, biologists different types of specimens, or business analysts different types of leaders.

This essay also gives you a choice of practicing either a thesis-driven organizational structure or an IMRD structure. These two organizational structures are among the most common in academic writing.

The Connected Curriculum: Designing a Vertical Transfer Writing Curriculum

DAN MELZER

Rebecca Nowacek (2011) observes that "scholarship on transfer in the field of rhetoric and composition has understandably focused on first year composition: what knowledge and abilities transfer out of, and less commonly, into FYC" (p. 99). There is consensus in this research that all too often students fail to transfer skills learned in their first-year composition courses to other writing contexts across the curriculum. There is also consensus that composition instructors wishing to encourage transfer should focus on metacognitive awareness of writing processes; understanding of key writing studies concepts like rhetorical situation, genre, and discourse community; and making explicit connections to students' future college and professional reading and writing tasks (Beaufort, 2007; Bergmann & Zepernick, 2007; Clark & Hernandez, 2011; Fishman & Reiff, 2008; Wardle, 2007). What scholars have focused less attention on is how these lessons learned from the research on transfer and first-year composition might inform the design not just of first-year composition courses, but of university writing across the curriculum (WAC) efforts, from a student's first year to his or her final semester. With the exception of Anne Beaufort (2007) and David Smit (2004), even researchers who have studied courses across disciplines have focused their advice not on the structural design of campus WAC programs, but on what individual instructors can do to encourage transfer (Caroll, 2002; Driscoll, 2011; Nowacek, 2011; Sternglass, 1997).

Writing program administrators (WPAs) interested in the issue of longitudinal design for college writing commonly draw on the concept of *vertical curriculum* (Crowley 1998; Hall, 2006; Jamieson, 2009; Miles et al; 2008). A vertical writing curriculum, with carefully sequenced writing courses in composition, general education, and the majors that connect to and build upon one another, certainly has transfer as an implicit goal. Discussions of vertical curriculum and discussions of transfer often occur on separate tracks and these two emerging areas of interest for writing studies would benefit from more explicit and in-depth connections.

This essay will make a stronger and more explicit connection between the scholarship on transfer and the scholarship on vertical writing by discussing the principles of a *vertical transfer writing curriculum*. I engage in theory-building by synthesizing the research on transfer and the discussions of vertical writing curriculum into a set of principles I hope will be useful in guiding the way WPAs design college writing programs ranging from the first year to the final semester. I begin with a brief overview of the literature on transfer and the literature on vertical writing curriculum, followed by a synthesis of the two areas of study in the form of a set of general principles for a vertical transfer writing curriculum. In order to make these abstract principles concrete, I discuss the redesign of the campus writing program at my institution, which has moved from a lateral curriculum that did not encourage transfer to a vertical curriculum that emphasizes transfer at each stage of students' careers as college writers.

Writing Transfer and the Vertical Writing Curriculum: An Overview and Synthesis

The following overview of the literature on writing transfer and the literature on the design of vertical writing curriculum is meant to be selective, not exhaustive. I highlight the features of transfer research that are: a) most commonly cited in research on transfer and writing, b) most relevant to the design of campus writing programs, and c) most useful in making connections between transfer and vertical curriculum design. I begin with a brief overview of the literature on transfer in general, and transfer and writing in particular.

The literature on transfer from the fields of educational psychology and writing studies is rich and complex, exploring everything from epistemological frameworks for transfer, categories of transfer, student disposition and transfer, and classroom practices. For the purposes of this essay, I will focus on aspects of transfer most often cited in the research on transfer and writing:

- Positive vs. negative transfer
- Threshold concepts and transfer
- Low road vs. high road transfer
- Metacognition and transfer
- Near vs. far transfer
- Vertical transfer

In order to discuss these transfer concepts in a concrete way, I use the example of a hypothetical student, Ling, as she moves from first-year composition to graduation.

Suppose that Ling had been taught to use the five-paragraph theme in her high school English classes, and she assumes that this format will also be expected in first-year composition. When Ling is asked to write a rhetorical analysis of an academic genre in her first-year composition class, she uses her default five-paragraph theme format and does poorly on the assignment. This is an example of *negative transfer*, in which learning from one situation interferes with learning from another situation (Schunk, 2004; Woltz et al., 2000). However, if Ling had written personal narratives in her high school English classes and then draws on her narrative writing skills to complete a literacy history narrative in her first-year composition class, she may experience *positive transfer*—learning from one situation assisting in another situation.

Another way of looking at Ling's conflict between the five-paragraph theme and the genre analysis assignment is with *threshold concepts*. A threshold concept is a key disciplinary concept that acts as a gateway to a discipline, opening up new ways of thinking about that discipline (Meyer & Land, 2006). David Perkins (2006) emphasizes that threshold concepts can be troubling to students, since they may be alien or counterintuitive, and may force students to give up previously held beliefs. A student like Ling who has been taught the five-paragraph theme in high school may struggle with the first-year composition threshold concept of *genre*, but an understanding of genre will help Ling cross the boundary from high school to college writing.

If Ling takes an introduction to biology general education course in her sophomore year and learns about the scientific method, and then draws on that knowledge to write a lab report in a chemistry class in her major a year later, she would be applying *high road* transfer. Perkins and Salomon (1989, "Rocky Roads") developed the constructs of *low road* versus *high road* transfer. Low road transfer occurs when students practice skills until they become routine and are triggered automatically and unconsciously. High road transfer, requiring less time and practice, involves abstracting from underlying principles. Rounsaville et al. (2012) further articulate high road transfer:

> "High road" transfer involves the deliberate, mindful abstraction of knowledge, skills, or strategies from one context to be re-localized and successfully leveraged in another, distinct context, and is distinguished by the learner's role in actively seeking connections between prior knowledge and new learning encounters. (para. 5)

If Ling learns to be a more self-reflective writer and to monitor and adjust her writing processes in first-year writing, she is more likely to achieve high road transfer. In a review of the transfer literature, Mikulecky et al. (1994) concludes that in the field of literacy study, metacognitive strategies such as setting goals and making predictions are examples of high road transfer. Dively and Nelms (2007) found that the ability to be a reflective writer was a key factor in successful transfer of knowledge from first-year composition to writing-intensive courses in the major. They argue that "reflection represents an important mechanism for achieving metacognitive awareness of the potential for transferring learning across contexts" (p. 216).

If the lab report Lynn is asked to write in her chemistry class is a new genre for her, and she uses the rhetorical analysis skills she learned in her first-year composition course to help her write the lab report, she is enacting *far transfer*. Far transfer involves the application of skills to a context that is further removed from the original context, and it is in contrast to *near transfer*, which occurs when there is a similar context for when a skill is first acquired and when it is applied again in another context (Royer, 1986). Context is a key word in the transfer literature: Foertsch (1995) argues that abstract rules should be taught in conjunction with concrete examples, and Berryman and Bailey (1992) claim that learning transfers best in real situations where knowledge and strategies are learned at the same time. Perkins and Salomon (1998) argue that one way to encourage transfer is "hugging," which means teaching a skill in the context of what we want it to transfer to. Researchers who study transfer would argue that if Ling was asked by her first-year composition instructor to mimic a genre in her future major, and Ling attempted to write a lab report, she would be less likely to achieve transfer than if she were writing the lab report in the context of a chemistry course.

Suppose Ling takes a capstone course in her major, and in her final essay she is asked to reflect on which thinking and writing skills she learned in her major will be most relevant to her career as a chemist. This would represent an attempt by Ling's instructor at encouraging *forward reaching* transfer (Perkins & Salomon, 1998). In forward reaching transfer students think about future contexts where a skill may be applied, and in *backward reaching* transfer students draw on prior knowledge and apply it to a current task, as in the example of Ling applying her knowledge of writing personal narratives in high school when writing a literacy history narrative in first-year composition.

As Ling moves from her first-year composition course to introductory courses in her major to capstone courses, she would ideally experience more and more complex and discipline-specific writing tasks, and she would draw on what she had learned previously each time she encountered a more difficult task. This would entail *vertical transfer*. Vertical transfer is transfer to a new learning situation that requires a higher order of thinking skills than would be necessary in a prior situation (Haskell, 2000). Vertical transfer is contrasted with *lateral transfer*, which involves transfer to related tasks that do not require new skills or more complex learning. Successful vertical transfer requires both prerequisite skills and the ability to construct new knowledge in new contexts. Gagne (1965) first developed the concept of vertical transfer, and he is one of the originators of vertical curriculum design. Gagne's work reminds us that in the design of campus writing programs we should consider not just the vertical nature of our curriculum, but also how to ensure transfer as students move vertically through the curriculum.

Although most writing studies scholars who have studied transfer have focused their attention on the design of first-year composition curriculum, a few scholars have drawn on the transfer research to sketch out more than a curriculum for first-year composition. Rather, they have outlined an entire university writing program. In *College Writing and Beyond*, Anne Beaufort (2007) makes an argument for developmental, sequenced sets of courses in the majors in order to move students toward increasing understanding of disciplinary subject matter, disciplinary genres, discourse community knowledge, and critical thinking. Beaufort references David Smit (2004), who in *The End of Composition Studies* argues for a carefully planned sequence of courses with "an increasing level of domain-specific knowledge" (185). Although Smit, like Beaufort, does not use the term *vertical curriculum*, his central focus is on rethinking entire university writing programs to ensure that writing in different courses is "more related and systematic, so that instructors can build on what students have learned previously" (p. 193). Smit argues that WAC/WID is the most effective tool for achieving this goal. The design of sequenced core courses in a hierarchy of thinking and writing skills that Beaufort and Smit argue for connects closely to Gagne's concept of vertical transfer.

Although concepts such as positive and negative transfer, low and high road transfer, near and far transfer, and vertical and lateral transfer are not often explicitly referenced in discussions of vertical writing curriculum, there is certainly an implicit connection between transfer concepts and principles of vertical writing curriculum design. For example, Miles et al. (2008) outlines guiding principles of a vertical curriculum that include recursion over time, so that concepts are introduced, practiced, and reinforced; a variety of "production-based" courses that combine experiential and academic learning; and the creation of sequences of courses that build upon one another (pp. 505-506). Like Miles et al., Jamieson (2009) recommends a vertical curriculum that emphasizes repeated writing opportunities throughout a student's career, required courses that focus on writing in the context of the discipline, and capstone courses with a research emphasis. The emphasis on recursion of skills and concepts in vertical curriculum design can be related to both low road and high road transfer and near and far transfer, and the emphasis on writing in the context of a discipline and on "production-based" and experiential writing echoes Perkins and Salomon's concept of hugging.

Like Beaufort and Smit, Hall (2006) proposes a continuous scale of goals that move toward more complexity and more discipline-specificity as students progress from first-year composition to capstone experiences in their major. Hall is interested in "the big picture of a student's academic development" (pp. 5-6), and argues for what he refers to as a *Unified Writing Curriculum*. Hall believes that each course in this unified sequence of introductory, advanced, and intermediate writing courses should have clear outcomes that build seamlessly toward disciplinary expertise. Hall feels that WAC should be concerned with "the vertical integration of writing instruction at various levels and at various times throughout the whole period of a student's undergraduate career" (p. 6).

Perkins and Salomon (1989) argue that transfer must be cued, primed, and guided (p. 19), and they claim that conditions for transfer can be engineered in the classroom. Like Miles et al., Jamieson, and Hall, my concern in this essay is not engineering the classroom, but the entire curriculum. I hope to add new dimensions to Miles et al., Jamieson, and Hall's visions of vertical curriculum design by explicitly integrating concepts from the literature on transfer into vertical curriculum design. Through an application of a synthesis of the research on transfer and vertical curriculum design, student writing can be cued and guided from the first year to the final semester, and transfer engineered not just from first-year writing to courses in the disciplines but at every stage of a student's college writing career. WPAs should focus their efforts not only on transfer from first-year writing, but also on what Perkins and Salomon (2012) call "the connected curriculum." To achieve vertical transfer in a campus writing program, I propose the following vertical writing transfer curriculum principles:

Require self-reflection and self-monitoring throughout the curriculum

Missing from discussions of vertical curriculum is an emphasis on teaching and practicing metacognition, and not only in first-year composition but also at every stage of students' academic writing careers. Since metacognitive awareness is key for successful transfer to more complex rhetorical situations, WPAs should work to ensure that there are moments of self-reflection built-in to core writing requirements and writing placement and assessment (Beaufort, 2007; Dively & Nelms, 2007; Mikulecky et al. 1994).

Distribute writing over time and embed writing throughout the curriculum

Vertical curriculum design emphasizes writing-intensive experiences at each stage of students' academic careers—from first-year composition, to general education, to introductions to the major, to capstone courses. The value of embedding these writing experiences in their disciplinary contexts is reinforced by the literature on transfer, which shows that students are more likely to learn something—and then transfer that learning to new situations—when the target learning outcome is embedded in disciplinary curriculum and practiced frequently (Beaufort, 2007; Perkins & Salomon, 1998; Smit, 2004).

Focus on situated, authentic, domain-specific practice

Vertical curriculum design makes the argument that first-year composition provides only an introductory domain for academic writing, and that writing must be situated in the disciplines and in experiential learning opportunities such as service learning and internships. In other words, first-year composition can introduce students to academic literacy threshold concepts like *revision, purpose, audience, genre,* and *discourse community*. However, these concepts need to be reinforced and further contextualized in specific disciplinary domains in general education and in the majors. Transfer is more likely to occur when learning is authentic and connected to disciplinary and professional practice (Berryman & Bailey, 1992; Foertsch, 1995; Perkins & Salomon, 1998).

Introduce and reinforce academic writing threshold concepts

Vertical curriculum design does not explicitly reference threshold concepts, but vertical planning for writing should include strategies for introducing students to academic writing threshold concepts and then reinforcing those concepts in future courses. Writing studies threshold concepts like *revision* and *genre* should be introduced in first-year composition and then reinforced in writing center tutoring, WAC faculty development efforts, and WAC initiatives such as writing fellows programs or writing-intensive courses. Vertical curriculum design should also consider where and when disciplinary threshold concepts would be introduced and reinforced in the majors (Meyer & Land, 2006; Perkins 2006).

Create shared writing meta-language

To achieve the goals of vertical design and the "connected curriculum," it is helpful to have a shared campus language regarding writing concepts and terms. Transfer is more likely to occur when instructors are using similar terms in similar ways as students move from first-year composition, to general education, and then to the majors.

Design multiple opportunities for peer mentoring

Guidance from more experienced peers can help students cross academic thresholds and can encourage forward-reaching transfer of writing skills from high school to first-year writing, from first-year writing to general education, and from general education to the majors. At the same time, when students take on the role of mentoring less experienced peers, they practice backward-reaching transfer and metacognitive awareness of the concepts they are teaching (Nowacek, 2011).

Designing a Vertical Transfer Writing Curriculum: An Example

The final section of this essay exemplifies the application of vertical transfer writing principles through a discussion of the revision of the campus writing program at my institution from a lateral writing curriculum to a vertical transfer curriculum.

There are endless ways to apply the vertical transfer writing curriculum principles I outlined in the previous section, and the form these principles may take in practice will always depend on local contexts. The point of my example is not to offer a list of writing program features that must be in place to achieve vertical transfer, but rather a concrete example to help readers imagine what a vertical transfer writing curriculum might look like at one institution—a large state comprehensive college in a diverse, urban environment.

Before a group of rhetoric and composition faculty at my institution were hired a decade ago and began making reforms to our campus writing program, students experienced negative transfer and little sense of vertical progression as they moved from first-year composition into general education and then into their majors. The point of entry to first-year composition was a Chancellor-mandated timed writing and multiple choice test which conflicted with the emphasis on writing as a social process in our first-year composition courses: the single draft, five-paragraph theme approach that students used in the timed exam had the effect of negative transfer when those same writing habits were applied by students to first-year composition assignments. Each second-semester composition course was based on a theme of the instructor's choosing, and because many instructors had a background in literature or creative writing this theme often focused on a novel. Students who applied the literary analysis and descriptive writing style they learned in the second-semester composition course to courses in general education or their major would experience negative transfer. Students were required to take only a single writing intensive course, inside or outside of their major, and quite often the students who needed the most practice with writing would delay taking the second-semester composition course and the writing intensive course until their final semester, which was possible due to a lack of regulation by academic affairs. A rising junior timed writing test had no connection to the writing intensive courses it was meant to place students into. There were no shared outcomes in the composition courses or the writing intensive courses, minimal faculty development for the teaching of writing, and little student support for writing beyond a small, underfunded writing center. In some ways my institution represented a worst-case scenario for transfer and vertical design, but readers may recognize some problematic elements listed here in their own campus writing programs.

There are multiple changes the WPAs at my institution made—and are currently still making—to move from negative transfer to positive transfer and from a lateral to a vertical curriculum. I will begin by simply listing the changes, and then discuss how they exemplify the vertical transfer writing curriculum principles I outlined in the previous section:

1. We received permission from the chancellor's office to replace the timed writing exam with Directed Self-Placement (DSP) to place students into first-year composition courses.
2. We changed the curriculum of the second-semester composition course to a WAC focus.
3. We created a proposal to give departments the option of becoming a writing intensive designated major (WID major), which means students who completed the major would satisfy their writing intensive requirement through taking a series of core courses in the major that emphasize sequenced writing experiences.
4. We created small-group, adjunct tutoring, one-unit courses for composition and for writing intensive courses led by advanced undergraduate and graduate students across disciplines.
5. We offered students one unit of credit for regular, weekly tutoring at the University Reading and Writing Center.
6. We offered classroom outreach workshops to instructors across disciplines on writing studies threshold concepts such as "revising vs. editing" and "peer response."
7. We created a junior-level writing-in-the-majors course taught by composition specialists.
8. We created a proposal for a required longitudinal career portfolio that would replace the rising junior timed-writing test.
9. We developed shared learning outcomes for first-year composition, second-semester composition, and writing intensive courses.
10. We hired a WAC coordinator and a writing assessment coordinator to help with WAC faculty development and university writing assessment.
11. We created a proposal for a yearly faculty development and writing assessment retreat for writing intensive teachers.
12. We created a university writing rubric and a university student writing guide.
13. We made the second-semester composition course a sophomore course and made it a prerequisite for the rising junior placement, and we convinced academic affairs to place registration holds on students who did not complete their rising junior placement by the end of their first semester as juniors.

Each of the changes listed above contributed to the movement from a lateral curriculum with serious problems of negative transfer to a vertical transfer writing curriculum. Below I discuss in more detail how the changes to the campus writing program at my institution reflect the vertical transfer writing curriculum principles I outlined in the previous section by revisiting each principle in light of the revised campus writing program.

Require self-reflection and self-monitoring throughout the curriculum

Timed writing tests require little self-reflection, but metacognition is built in to DSP. In our DSP materials students are asked to take a literacy self-survey in which they reflect on their strengths and weaknesses as writers, and are also asked to consider their high school literacy experiences (backward reaching transfer) and analyze the kinds of writing they will be asked to do in our first-year composition courses (forward reaching transfer). As part of the proposed rising junior portfolio placement, students must include a cover letter where they assess what they've learned about writing in college thus far, and consider their strengths and weaknesses as writers as they enter their major. Teaching activities that require students to reflect on their writing—and to use writing as a tool for metacognition—are discussed in WAC faculty development activities and will be encouraged as the WAC and writing assessment coordinator work with departments on becoming certified as WID majors.

Distribute writing over time and embed writing throughout the curriculum

Students will have at least one writing intensive experience every year in our revised campus writing program: first-year composition, sophomore composition, and a series of core courses in their major as our institution moves toward the embedded model of WID majors. The adjunct nature of the small group tutoring and University Reading and Writing Center tutoring courses ensures *hugging*—writing practice and feedback in domain-specific contexts, and especially the context of writing in a specific major. Prerequisites and enforcement of registration holds for students who are not following the sequence will help insure that writing intensive experiences are distributed over time and not put off until just before a student is preparing to graduate.

Focus on situated, authentic, domain-specific practice

Instructors in the WAC-focused sophomore composition course attempt to give students an authentic bridge to general education by asking students to analyze the ways of making meaning, formal conventions, research methods, etc. of different academic discourse communities using actual writing assignments and examples of student and professional writing. A junior-level writing-in-the-majors course uses the same forward-reaching transfer strategies as the sophomore course, but is focused on students exploring the writing done in their majors. The writing intensive requirement is slowly shifting from students frequently taking a writing intensive course outside their discipline to a series of courses within a discipline, and adjunct tutoring support for writing intensive courses focuses entirely on workshops of the papers students are assigned in their writing intensive courses.

Introduce and reinforce academic writing threshold concepts

Students are first introduced to writing studies threshold concepts like *revision* and *genre* in the DSP materials, and these concepts are emphasized in the shared learning outcomes for first-year and sophomore composition courses. The composition courses require that instructors use the university student writing guide, which also focuses on writing studies threshold concepts. Although there are not assurances that instructors in the disciplines will introduce students to and then reinforce disciplinary threshold concepts, moving the writing intensive requirement to a series of core courses in the major makes it more likely that disciplinary threshold concepts will be taught and practiced through the use of writing, and provides an opportunity for the writing assessment coordinator to discuss threshold concepts with departments as she works with them on curriculum mapping.

Create shared writing meta-language

Although Anson et al. (2012) make a convincing argument against generic university writing rubrics in favor of discipline and course-specific rubrics, the creation of a university writing rubric does help promote writing meta-language: the university writing rubric discusses writing concepts like *revision, audience,* and *editing.* This meta-language is also used in the student writing handbook, and it appears throughout the shared learning outcomes for both the composition courses and the writing intensive courses. University Reading and Writing Center tutors and the tutors who facilitate the small group adjunct tutoring also use this meta-language when helping student writers, as it is reinforced in their tutor training. The writing meta-language is reinforced again in classroom outreach workshops offered by the center, and in faculty development workshops and seminars offered by the WAC program.

Design multiple opportunities for peer mentoring

A large percentage of students receive regular peer mentoring, whether it is in a small group workshop or one-on-one conferences an hour a week with a tutor in the University Reading and Writing Center. Nowacek (2011) argues that tutors' central charge is to "facilitate the transfer of writing-related knowledge for student writers," and that as they do this they develop a greater capacity to see connections in their own writing (p. 136). The students receiving tutoring in our writing program receive reinforcement of forward-reaching transfer from more experienced peers, and the tutors—who include students from across disciplines—gain metacognitive awareness of their writing processes and the rhetoric of their disciplines through the act of tutoring student writers. At many institutions faculty and/or professional staff tutor students one-on-one or in small groups, and this structure also benefits students in regards to transfer, but peer tutoring has the added benefit of the student tutors gaining metacognitive awareness of their writing processes.

The changes described above represent an attempt to move from negative transfer to positive transfer and from a lateral writing curriculum to a vertical transfer curriculum, but there are certainly more changes to be made that could help with transfer. The current junior-level writing-in-the-majors course taught by a composition specialist should aid with transfer as students cross the threshold into their majors, but the literature on transfer supports the WID argument that a course that introduces a student to writing in his or her major should be taught by a disciplinary specialist in that major. The embedded model of the WID major is more likely to result in positive transfer than a single writing-intensive course, but an additional requirement of a capstone course in each major would help to ensure vertical transfer. Universal service learning and internship requirements would also improve the chances of transfer for our students.

As my institution fully implements the vertical transfer writing curriculum model, it will be important to assess the extent to which students are transferring writing knowledge, habits, and skills at each stage in the curriculum. Research on transfer and writing supports the vertical transfer principles I propose, but more longitudinal writing research like Beaufort's (2007) that is explicitly focused on transfer not just from first-year composition but from each new threshold students cross in a vertical curriculum is needed. In the future, I hope to move beyond theory-building and examine portfolio cover letters from first-year composition, sophomore composition, the rising junior portfolio placement, and writing intensive courses to provide more substance to my argument for these vertical transfer writing curriculum principles—or to rethink these principles.

Whatever types of programs and courses an institution enacts to encourage vertical transfer, the important consideration is building them in to the core requirements of students' academic careers. Brent (2011) argues that successful transfer involves enculturating students into "long-standing mental habits, or dispositions" (p. 411). The mental habits and dispositions for transfer of writing begin with first-year composition, and the data from studies of what and how much students transfer from first-year composition to future courses is valuable in helping WPAs redesign first-year composition courses to encourage transfer. However, it's equally important that WAC theorists and practitioners extend the conversation on transfer well beyond first-year composition. Imagining core curriculum that will encourage vertical transfer is one way we can promote transfer of writing beyond first-year composition.

References

Anson, C. et al. (2012). Big rubrics and weird genres: The futility of using generic assessment tools across diverse instructional contexts. *Journal of Writing Assessment, 5*(1). Retrieved from http://www.journalofwritingassessment.org/article.php?article=57

Beaufort, A. (2007). *College writing and beyond: A new framework for university writing instruction*. Logan, UT: Utah State UP.

Bergmann, L., & Zepernick, J. (2007). Disciplinarity and transfer: Students' perceptions of learning to write. *Writing Program Administration, 31*(1-2), 124-49.

Berryman, S. E., & Bailey, T. R. (1992). *The double helix of education and the economy*. New York: Columbia University.

Brent, D. (2011). Transfer, transformation, and rhetorical knowledge: Insights from transfer theory. *Journal of Business and Technical Communication, 25*(4), 396-420.

Caroll, L. (2002). *Rehearsing new roles: How college students develop as writers*. Carbondale, IL: Southern Illinois University Press.

Clark, I. L., & Hernandez, A. (2011). Genre awareness, academic argument, and transferability. *The WAC Journal, 22*, 65-78.

Crowley, S. (1998). *Composition in the university: Historical and polemical essays*. Pittsburgh: University of Pittsburgh Press.

Dively, R. L., & Nelms, G. (2007). Perceived roadblocks to transferring knowledge from first-year composition to writing-intensive major courses: A pilot study. *Writing Program Administration, 31*(1-2), 214-240.

Driscoll, D. (2011). Connected, disconnected, or uncertain: Student attitudes about future writing contexts and perceptions of transfer from first-year writing to the disciplines. *Across the Disciplines, 8*(2). Retrieved from http://wac.colostate.edu/atd/articles/driscoll2011/

Fishman, J., & Reiff, M. J. (2008). Taking the high road: Teaching for transfer in an FYC program. *Composition Forum, 18*. Retrieved from http://compositionforum.com/issue/18/tennessee.php

Foertsch, J. (1995). Where cognitive psychology applies: How theories about memory and transfer can influence composition pedagogy. *Written Communication, 12*(3), 360-383.

Gagne, R. M. (1965). *The conditions of learning*. New York: Holt, Rinehart and Winston.

Hall, J. (2006). Toward a unified writing curriculum: Integrating WAC/WID with freshman composition. *The WAC Journal, 17*, 5-22.

Haskell, R. (2000). *Transfer of Learning: Cognition and Instruction*. San Diego: Academic Press

Jamieson, S. (2009). The vertical writing curriculum. In J. C. Post & J. A. Inman (Eds.), *Composition(s) in the new liberal arts* (pp. 159-184). Creskill, N.J.: Hampton.

Meyer, J., & Land, R. (Eds.). (2006). *Overcoming barriers to student understanding: Threshold concepts and troublesome knowledge*. New York: Routledge.

Mikulecky et al. (1994). *Literacy transfer: A review of the literature*. Philadelphia: National Center of Adult Literacy.

Miles, L. et al. (2008). Thinking vertically. *College Composition and Communication, 59*(3), 503-511.

Nowacek, R. (2011). *Agents of Integration: Understanding Transfer as a Rhetorical Act.* Carbondale, IL: Southern Illinois University Press.

Perkins, D. (2006). Constructivism and troublesome knowledge. In J. Meyer & R. Land (Eds.). *Overcoming barriers to student understanding: Threshold concepts and troublesome knowledge* (pp. 33-47). New York: Routledge.

Perkins, D., & Salomon, G. (1989). Are cognitive skills context bound? *Educational Researcher, 18*(1), 16-25.

—. (1989). Rocky roads to transfer: Rethinking mechanisms of a neglected phenomenon. *Educational Psychologist, 24*(2), 113-142.

—. (2012). The science and art of transfer. Retrieved from http:// learnweb.harvard.edu/alps/thinking/docs/trancost.htm

—. (1988). Teaching for transfer. *Educational Leadership, 46*(1), 22-32.

Rounsaville, A., Goldberg, R., & Bawarshi, A. (2008). From incomes to outcomes: FYW students' prior genre knowledge, meta-cognition, and the question of transfer. *Writing Program Administration, 32*(1), 97-112.

Royer, J. M. (1986). Designing instruction to produce understanding: An approach based on cognitive theory. In G. D. Phye & T. Andre (Eds.), *Cognitive classroom learning: Understanding, thinking, and problem solving* (pp. 83-113). Orlando: Academic Press.

Schunk, D. (2004). *Learning theories: An educational perspective*. Cambridge: Cambridge UP.

Smit, D. (2004). *The end of composition studies*. Carbondale, IL: Southern Illinois University Press.

Sternglass, M. (1997). *Time to know them: A longitudinal study of writing and learning at the college level*. Mahwah, N.J.: Lawrence Erlbaum Associates.

Wardle, E. (2007). Understanding "transfer" from FYC: Preliminary results of a longitudinal study. *Writing Program Administration, 31*(1-2), 65-85.

Woltz, D. J. et al. (2000). Negative transfer errors in sequential cognitive skills: Strong-but-wrong sequence application. *Journal of Experimental Psychology: Learning, Memory, and Cognition, 26*(3), 601-635.

Transfer and the Transformation of Writing Pedagogies in a Mathematics Course

SARAH BRYANT, NOREEN LAPE, AND JENNIFER SCHAEFER

When it comes to developing a WAC/WID program, the final frontier may very well be the mathematics department. Writing in the discipline—in this case, proof writing—involves a highly specialized language of symbolic notation accessible only to those fluent in that language (Parker and Mattison 39). When working with mathematics faculty to develop writing-intensive courses, writing program administrators face a unique challenge: that mathematics writing is not "writing" in the conventional sense and so traditional best practices do not directly apply. In other words, invention techniques like freewriting and cubing, structured in their usual way, may not be as useful to mathematics writers as they are to writers in other disciplines—such as English, history, and sociology—that are not as positivistic. In terms of revision, given that proof writing is less subjective than most other kinds of academic writing, peer review runs the risk of becoming an empty exercise in which unknowledgeable students provide equally unknowledgeable students with faulty feedback. And if, instead, the task of providing feedback is left to the professor who corrects the errors in the proof, there is nothing left for the writer to "re-see" and to revise. Instead, the developing proof writer must learn to transfer the feedback from one proof and apply it to a different proof of a similar genre.

In this essay, two mathematics professors and a writing program administrator will explain how we addressed these valid discipline-specific concerns when we collaborated to re-envision an introduction to proofs course as writing-intensive. In his history of the WAC Movement, David R. Russell notes, "mathematics has been a leader" among "discipline-specific movements to incorporate writing in teaching" (320). Over the years, a spate of essays on writing and mathematics has appeared in journals in the fields of writing studies, mathematics, and mathematics education. Several of these essays focus on using writing to learn, arguing in different ways that writing helps students more effectively process and comprehend mathematical concepts (Shepard; Estes; Ganguli; Shibli; McCormick; Grossman et al.; Flesher; Bahls, "Math"). Others illustrate how mathematics instructors can implement WAC techniques like peer review (Fernsten; Gopen and Smith), journaling (Mower), and informal expressive writing assignments (Cherkas; Bahls "Metaphor"). Patrick Bahls has written extensively on the connection between mathematics writing and WAC techniques. His book, *Student Writing in the Quantitative Disciplines*, is meant "to help faculty in the quantitative disciplines see how writing figures prominently in the learning process" (ix). The book contains chapters on the writing process, assessing and responding to student learning, and formal and informal writing assignments. These scholars demonstrate how mathematics instructors can *transport* writing pedagogies into the mathematics classroom.

We will argue that to enhance learning, mathematics instructors must *transform* writing pedagogies to fit the genre of proof writing. We see this as a necessary extension of WAC/WID pedagogy. In his cogent historical analysis, Russell points out the "split" between general composition courses that deliberately sought to develop students' writing skills and specialized courses in the discipline that presumed "writing acquisition" was "unconscious" (28). As a result, the disciplines did not find it "necessary to examine, much less improve, the way students are initiated into their respective symbolic universes" (30). We not only consider the truly symbolic universe of mathematics writing, but we go even further, and consider how students are initiated into the discipline by examining how the writing process, particularly the invention and revision stages, maps onto an introductory proofs course. As Bahls observes, "the steps of [the writing] process may take different forms for different kinds of writing, and for different disciplines" (*Student* 25). As we have experienced, the writing process, with its roots in the humanities, is not entirely congruent with the proof-writing genre. We will show how we transformed the writing process, particularly the invention and revision stages, by 1.) implementing structured, genre-specific heuristics for the invention stage; 2.) modifying peer-review techniques to support the revision stage of proof writing; and 3.) instituting metacognitive journals with the goal of aiding "high-road" knowledge transfer.

An Introductory Proofs Course: Before and After WAC

The traditional model for teaching mathematics reflects the well-known maxim of the famous mathematician Paul Halmos: "the best way to learn [mathematics] is to do [mathematics]" (466). Many students learn to "do mathematics" by completing homework sets and taking short quizzes to check for major gaps in understanding. Since repeated practice is the key to mastering exams, students quickly learn that success results from "doing more problems." In the early 2000s, the mathematics faculty at Dickinson College decided that simply doing more problems was not enough; students needed direct instruction on how to write mathematical arguments. The faculty identified specific areas of deficiency that encompassed both higher and lower order writing skills. In terms of higher order skills, students had difficulty knowing when and how to apply the appropriate proof techniques, and identifying logical gaps or mistakes that render a proof invalid; in terms of lower order skills, students struggled with composing explanations that were concise and communicated clearly to a reader, naming the variables according to mathematical convention, and constructing complete and connected sentences (as opposed to bullet points or fragments). A representative example comes from the work of Alice, one of Jennifer's students, who attempted to prove across several drafts that the product of any two consecutive integers is even. The first sentence of her lengthier first draft reads:

> Suppose l and m are two consecutive integers such that $l=r$ and $m=q+1$.

This first version contains both higher and lower order problems. The higher issue is that Alice's definitions for l and m, namely that $l=r$ and $m=q+1$, do not support her assumption that l and m are consecutive and so her subsequent argument is illogical. The lower issue is that Alice's writing lacks concision because she uses more variables than is conventional; she need only use m. Making an attempt to correct her errors, Alice produces the following:

> Suppose l and m are two consecutive integers such that $l=n$ and $m=n+1$.

In her revision, Alice uses the correct definition of consecutive integers: n and $n+1$. However, she continues to use more variables than is conventional. In her final revision of this sentence, she addresses all of the concerns:

> Suppose m and $m+1$ are two consecutive integers.

While this is a simple example, it is a common one that illustrates the kinds of higher and lower order thinking mathematics students must activate as they practice revision. Yet many students do not recognize the difference between higher and lower order concerns and so they do not know how to prioritize during the revision process.

Motivated to address these issues, the mathematics faculty decided to give proof writing more attention earlier in the curriculum. At the same time, there arose a college-wide initiative to develop writing-intensive courses in every major. The mathematics and computer science department responded by designating the introductory proofs course—in our curriculum discrete mathematics—as writing-intensive. Aiming to provide an effective gateway to the mathematics major, this course not only emphasizes discrete mathematics—including properties of numbers, sets, and functions—but also focuses on the art of writing mathematical arguments.

At first, mathematics faculty struggled to implement the criteria for writing-intensive courses in a way that made sense to them. The writing-intensive courses at our college combine WID and WAC learning goals: students learn the genres and conventions of the discipline (WID) and develop a functional writing process

(WAC). The mathematics and computer science department adopted Susanna Epps's *Discrete Mathematics and Applications*, a textbook whose rich resources and exercises on proofreading and the writing process address both goals. Complementing the student learning outcomes for the course, Epps's textbook covers the main genres of direct and indirect proofs. While faculty felt comfortable teaching disciplinary writing conventions, helping students develop a more functional writing process proved more problematic. Instructors incorporated an assortment of writing-related assignments and activities: for example, one created an in-house guide called "The Nuts and Bolts of Writing Mathematics," and others tried to implement revision exercises. Despite their efforts, instructors sensed the disconnection between writing and content instruction, and they struggled to develop a pedagogy that supported content and authentically incorporated the writing process as a means to developing stronger proof writers.

We began tackling the incongruence of proof writing with the process goals of writing-intensive courses in faculty development workshops. At Dickinson College, those teaching writing-intensive courses are invited to a half-day workshop entitled "Teaching the Writing-Intensive Course." This workshop draws faculty from across the disciplines and begins with a discussion of disciplinary genres and conventions before focusing on pedagogical skills like creating clear assignment prompts, designing an effective peer review, developing rubrics, and responding to writing assignments. After this workshop, faculty often elect to have follow-up consultations on course-specific concerns. Given the challenges that mathematics faculty were facing with authentically incorporating the writing process, we chose to meet and discuss how these techniques could be adapted to mathematical writing. This training and collaboration allowed us to prepare a course that fully integrated invention, peer review, revision, portfolios, and journals in a way that supported the development of proof writers. By taking full advantage of faculty development resources, we discovered new tools in the form of writing process pedagogy that truly helped our students *do* mathematics.

Transforming Invention Techniques

As we worked together to make the course writing-intensive, we grappled openly with a central question: is it helpful for mathematics writers to engage in the writing process—inventing, drafting, revising, and editing—when they are composing a mathematical proof? A mathematical proof "is a step-by-step logical or computational justification of a mathematical assertion, often drawing on prior proofs for its logical force" (Bahls, *Student* 22). Thus, prompts are not conducive to open-ended invention techniques like brainstorming or clustering. Consider the following prompt which is typical in an introductory proof-writing course:

Prove the following theorem: The sum of any two odd integers is even.

Since a proof is a written argument, to tackle this writing assignment, students must learn the content knowledge that would enable them to understand this statement, determine what makes the statement true, and then use logic to prove it. Traditionally, mathematics instructors would teach proof writing by demonstrating proofs—that is, composing perfectly formulated arguments on the board while their students watched in awe, marveling at the mystery. We wanted to figure out how to demystify proof writing by directly teaching disciplinary conventions that professional mathematicians have internalized. While the textbook explicitly covers logic, mathematical vocabulary, relevant theorems, and proof techniques, we wanted to teach the writing process and rhetorical situation. We began by focusing on the invention stage.

In *Student Writing in the Quantitative Disciplines*, Bahls recommends conventional invention techniques like freewriting, clustering, and cubing (24-29). While Bahls' techniques reflect the best practices of writing pedagogy, they are of limited use for proof writers because they do not take into account the highly specialized nature of the genre. For example, when describing freewriting, Bahls directs the writer to "gran[t] herself a fixed amount of time . . . during which she will write, nonstop, about a particular topic" (26). In mathematics writing, "scratch work" is the authentic equivalent of freewriting in which the writer works and reworks a shorthand version of a proof, including relevant terms, until she can visualize the end of the proof and the potential problem areas. Offering another traditional technique, Bahls defines cubing as a prewriting "tool designed to help writers examine a topic from every several [sic] different perspectives before writing about it more fully" (27). Bahls identifies "six faces of a cube": "describe it," "compare it," "associate it," "analyze it," "apply it," and "argue for or against it" (27). Conversely, we propose a new cube with discipline-specific prompts that scaffold the authentic invention process of mathematicians.

Table 1. Example Cube for Theorem: The sum of any two odd integers is even.

Invention Prompt	Pedagogy	Student Response
Summarize it.		
From a logical viewpoint, what does the theorem state?	Instructors teach symbolic logic and the logic of quantified statements during the first several weeks of class. Symbolic logic is the starting point for summarizing and categorizing statements.	Students should be able to summarize that the theorem is a statement about sums of any two odd integers. They should recognize that it is a universal statement and can be rewritten with logical quantifiers and variables. *For all integers m and n, if m and n are odd, then m+n is even.*
Unpack it.		
What are the key terms?	Instructors teach definitions so that students develop fluency in the underlying language of mathematics.	Students identify the key terms "integer," "odd," and "even." Students should rephrase those terms in mathematical language. For example: *Let n be an odd integer. Then n=2k+1 for some integer. k*
Delimit it.		
Given the logical form and key definitions, what is the appropriate starting and ending point for the proof?	Instructors model examples of how to begin and conclude a proof, often the most difficult skill for students. On assessments, instructors prompt students to "state the starting and ending point for this proof" to reinforce the importance of this step.	A student should know to start with the assumption that m and n are arbitrary odd integers and know the proof should conclude with $m+n$ is an even integer.
Analyze it.		
Is the theorem true or false? Is the theorem's validity based on previous results?	After delimiting the statement, the beginning and end may not be straightforward to connect. Instructors demonstrate for the class how a mathematician develops counterexamples and explores the consequences of the veracity of a given statement—a skill that is especially important for the theorems that are not self-evident. This exploration is part of a trained mathematician's thought process and must be explicitly taught to beginning proof writers.	Students should realize that the theorem is true and its proof is straightforward. In this case, the definitions lend themselves to a sketch of the proof, easily verifying its validity.

Frame it.		
What is the best proof technique for the theorem?	Instructors teach the structure of each proof technique, when to use a specific one, and discipline-specific conventions (e.g., always do a direct proof, rather than indirect, when possible).	The student must consider the various proof techniques. Based on their scratch work, it should be apparent that a direct proof is possible and, therefore, preferable for this theorem.
Make it appeal to an audience.		
Who is your peer audience? Which steps used in the analysis are necessary and sufficient to convince them?	Instructors implement collaborative peer groups to make proof writers aware of audience. The students advance from the notion that a proof must be complete and omit no details to a more mathematically-sophisticated understanding of what is and is not common knowledge for an audience. By writing for an audience, clarity, conciseness, and exposition become integral to the proof, rather than afterthoughts.	The students should understand that the audience expects every step of this proof to be justified, as these steps constitute the argument itself.

The first column in the cube identifies questions we want proof writers to ask themselves in the invention stage. Rather than adopting open-ended and unspecific questions like "What can it be used for?" and "What are its inner workings?" (Bahls 27), this column identifies discipline-specific questions for proof writers. Assuming that instructors will directly teach the logic and mathematical content that writers need to invent proofs, the second column offers specific prompts to help the instructor guide the students as they address the question in the first column. The third column provides an example of a student response to the parity theorem mentioned above. While this theorem is a simple example, the questions are transferable to more complex theorems in advanced courses.

Transforming the Revision Process

Having re-imagined invention in a disciplinary context, we realized that revision as practiced in traditional writing courses would have to be adapted to fit a proof-writing course. In a traditional writing course, writers receive feedback from peers and/or the instructor and then use that feedback to produce a new and, ideally, improved version of the draft. In applying this model of revision to proof-writing assignments, we grappled with the argument of a colleague in mathematics who asserted that revision does not work in a proof-writing course because the instructor could not provide feedback on a proof without also revealing the answer to the proof. And once the instructor provided that feedback, there was no need for the student to do the problem again. Instead, the instructor would expect students to apply his feedback to the next proof, making "repetition," rather than revision, the goal. His comment raised several important questions for us. Would students better learn how to write proofs by repeating problem types, by revising one particular problem, or by practicing a combination of the two? Could peer reviewers give feedback—possibly even more effectively than professors—by virtue of the peer reviewers' novice positions? Or would unknowledgeable peers end up offering equally unknowledgeable peers faulty feedback? We resolved the repetition versus revision debate by having the students practice both—that is, revisit the same *genre* in homework problems and revise the same *problem* for final portfolios. On the one hand, when we assigned homework problems, we assumed the role of "expert correctors" in order to give students written feedback on the logic and rhetoric of their proofs. After receiving the comments, students would repeat the process, completing more problems until "practice made perfect." On the other hand, we instituted peer review because we saw the value of students' drafting, collaborating, and then revising the same proof as they constructed their portfolios. To that end, we assigned students to peer review groups at the beginning of the semester. When we posted daily homework problems, we also listed additional "portfolio problems" of the same type. Students selected and completed as many as three portfolio problems, which they submitted for daily peer review. At first, peer review was very difficult for them. Rather than unknowledgeable peers leading each other astray with bad advice, they would write superficial comments on each other's papers and then sit quietly together, engaging in very little discussion about their drafts. As a result, we revised our pedagogy and started teaching students how to engage in peer review. We would analyze sample proofs and apply tips gathered from multiple sources, including the rich guide on mathematical writing by Knuth, Larrabee and Roberts (4). As the students learned how to revise, they began focusing on a different group member's paper each day and their discussions began to evince more critical thinking.

We learned that peer review was effective, not just because it provided direct feedback for the writer but because it enabled the writer to re-see his own writing through that of his peers. Writers reported benefitting from conversations with their peers, as in the case of one student whose peer "helped give me ideas on how to better format one of my problems in my portfolio." This writer concluded, "As with all writings it's important to receive feedback to better the quality of the writings." More interestingly, several writers found peer review helpful because it created transfer experiences, enabling them to re-see their own work through the lens of their peers' work. One wrote, "There was an interesting peer reviewing incident where I and one of my peers both made the mistake of thinking that a statement was false and proceeding to provide identical counterexamples to disprove the statement. During the review, we both noticed each other's mistake and deduced where we went wrong." While this writer viewed the proof as a mathematical problem, using terms like "disprove the statement" and "mistake," two others viewed their proofs in writerly terms. One student wrote:

> Peer review was really helpful for me because it gave me an opportunity to see how other people approach the same problems. Not only was seeing other people's approach to the math portion helpful, especially with more complex proofs, but it was also helpful to see the *different ways people wrote*. There were some problems where I felt like *I just couldn't articulate* what I needed to in order to complete the proof. After reading over some of the solutions from my peer review group, however, I was able to figure out *what I was trying to say* and improve my own work. Being exposed to my *peers' writing styles* allowed me to regularly *reevaluate my own*, which has, I think, made me a better proof writer.

Another student explained:

> Among the many things I learned during peer review, the most valuable was learning *alternate ways to write our work*. Since so much of discrete mathematics relies on our *wording, clarity, and organization of problems*, it was extremely useful to see other's work and learn and share *better ways of expressing solutions*. (emphasis added)

Peer review showed these two writers "different ways people wrote" so that they could better "express" or "articulate" solutions. The second writer, in particular, uses writerly terms like "wording, clarity, and organization" to describe the proof-writing process. Both writers viewed revision as a writing, rather than a mathematical task, and they valued peer review because it enabled *transfer*: the ability to think about one's learning and to abstract from that learning principles that can be applied to another context (Salomon and Perkins). A fourth student states the transfer benefit most clearly: "It was also somewhat helpful to be able to look at someone else's proof and pickout mistakes because then I could transfer those kinds of objective thoughts when I looked at my own proofs" [sic]. In fact, when designing the writing-intensive component of this course, Sarah and Jennifer identified transfer as a major goal. In peer review, these four students practiced the "mindful abstracting of knowledge" from one context (their peers' papers) for use in another context (their own papers) (Salomon and Perkins 115). As such, rather than receiving direct critiques from peer reviewers, these writers engaged in the more complex task of critiquing a peer's draft, abstracting a mathematical principle, formulating their own feedback, and using it to revise their own writing. Far from misleading, peer review sharpened writers' critical reading and logical reasoning skills and helped them take ownership of their own work.

Teaching Metacognition and Aiding Transfer

These transfer moments were not just "happy accidents." Instead, writers were required to keep journals and regularly respond to metacognitive prompts created to aid the transfer of learning. In designing the journal assignment, we followed the advice of Anne Beaufort for "increasing the chances of transfer of learning" and taught learners "the practice of mindfulness or meta-cognition." Beaufort describes metacognition as "vigilant attentiveness to a series of high-level questions as one is in the process of writing" (Beaufort 152). To support knowledge transfer, students wrote at least one journal entry per week, summarizing a learning moment that they experienced. In addition, throughout the semester, they responded to specific prompts—what Beaufort calls high-level questions—that we created to help them reflect on the writing process and articulate abstract concepts regarding mathematical logic and methods of proof. The following is a sampling of our journal questions:

> Could you have found the answer by doing something different? What?
>
> Where else could you use this type of problem solving?
>
> What other strategies could you use to solve this problem?
>
> Write four steps for somebody else that will be solving this problem.
>
> What would you like to do better next time?
>
> What is one thing you have learned or changed because of peer-review feedback?
>
> Based on the feedback you have gotten on your homework, at what stage(s) in the proof-writing process can you make improvements?

Because we wanted this writing to be meaningful, we provided handouts on how to journal, and we intermittently collected the journals to make sure that students were being faithful scribes.

Given the time and effort students and instructors put into the creation of these journals, we wanted to know if writers benefitted from keeping a journal in a mathematics class or if the journal was nothing more than "busy work." Specifically, we combed the journals for evidence of transfer only to discover students reporting several varieties of transfer experiences related to both mathematical and writing contexts. In their oft-cited article on transfer mechanisms, Gavriel Salomon and David N. Perkins distinguish between forward-reaching and backward-reaching high-road transfer. According to Salomon and Perkins, in forward-reaching transfer, "the general formulation occurs initially and finds new application spontaneously later. One might say that during the initial learning it became set up for later spontaneous use ...". (119). One student, we will call her Amy, anticipated forward-reaching transfer of mathematical principles when she observed of her discrete mathematics course: "This is sort of the beginning/basis for most future math classes; I hear that many of the coming courses are very much based on proofs, and having learned the basics and techniques of proof writing, this will clearly help in the future." While Amy understands that she will have to draw on her learning in other mathematics courses, Suhil explains how his knowledge of calculus from a previous semester helped him solve a proof by induction in discrete mathematics. In a detailed journal entry, Suhil explains his experience of backward-reaching high-road transfer:

> While working through proof 5.4.7 to create a strong induction proof for the portfolio (I had realized that I had none that I was really proud of), I had hit a wall. I couldn't find a way to get rid of a $k\text{-}1$ subscript, and by this change from the recursive definition to the explicit definition of the equation, via substitution or any other clear technique. I had worked around the algebra for a while, working in circles for an extended period of time. Giving up on simply trying to solve it, I strategized.

Suhil experiments with some deductions and revisits his assumptions until he abstracts a principle from calculus, a course he had taken in an earlier semester. He continues, "Then, after looking into my algebra again, an idea from an integration by parts (my personal favorite integration technique) problem I had solved over a year ago came to me." After describing his mathematical reasoning in detail, he articulates the abstract principle: "The concept of needing to go back to the beginning in order to progress in some problems stuck with me. In this case, the 'a-ha' moment was realizing that I could work several steps backwards because of strong induction." Thus, Suhil experiences backward-reaching high-road transfer as he "formulates an abstraction guiding his . . . reaching back to past experience for relevant connections"—in this case, his abstractions from calculus enable him to revise his algebraic proof (Salomon and Perkins 119).

Other students, who spoke about the development of writing processes and skills, commented on how the lessons could be transferred not only to other mathematics courses but also to other disciplinary writing situations. Julie reflected on her struggle with "rational and irrational numbers." She learned that by

> building on the integer proofs by contradiction and understanding the theorem that stated the irrationality of square root of two, I could figure out where I needed to manipulate the math in order to reach a contradiction. This sort of consciousness about the problem is necessary for doing proofs

by induction, which require scratch work in order to figure out the more complicated conclusions necessary for my proof by strong induction.

Julie has awareness not only of the kind of "consciousness" she needs to write mathematically but also of the mathematical writing process, one that "require[s] scratch work." While Julie has developed process knowledge that will help her in subsequent mathematics courses, Adam imagines that what he learned about writing might be transferable to other disciplines: "This class may help with my essay writing as well in terms of planning, organization, and conciseness." Finally, Xiying anticipates the transfer of a general writing skill, concision, to other contexts: "Furthermore, the course has helped me improve upon basic writing skills, most notably my ability to be concise. In writing proofs, any extra wording often times detracts from the proof, thus one is forced to be concise." In figuring out how to eliminate extra wording from her writing, Xiying has developed an aspect of her writing style that will serve her well when she writes in other disciplines.

In telling the story of collaboration between two mathematics professors and a writing program director, we offer a writing pedagogy specifically tailored to writers of mathematics. At the same time, we also suggest how students who learn this specialized form of writing can be taught to think about the transfer of knowledge. The voices of writers captured in their journals speak strongly of their ability to imagine how their learning applies to different contexts both near and far—from subsequent courses in the mathematics curriculum to writing assignments in other disciplines.

Beyond the reflections students offered in their class journals, we want to know if students continued to transfer what they learned about the writing process to writing assignments in other classes—both within and outside of the mathematics department. To that end, we have fashioned a multipart assessment project. First, we will survey students about whether they continued to use writing process skills—like "scratch work," "cubing," peer review, and revision—when writing proofs for subsequent courses. Next, we will convene a focus group of students and ask them to share and discuss artifacts that exemplify these skills. A benefit of teaching at a small liberal arts college and having close relationships with students is that these kinds of assessment projects are feasible. Finally, focusing on mathematics majors and minors, we will compare the overall mathematics grade point averages of students in Jennifer's Discrete Mathematics course from 2008 with students in Jennifer and Sarah's WAC/WID transformed version of the course. By using a variety of assessment tools, we will determine whether or not students transferred the WAC/WID skills they learned in the course and improved their ability to write proofs.

Finally, we offer a lesson to WAC/WID directors about the importance of creating knowledge transfer opportunities in faculty development contexts. For WAC/WID directors, a major challenge when it comes to faculty development involves making disciplinary conventions explicit for faculty who do not routinely teach writing and who have internalized those conventions. Yet, in the words of Jennifer and Sarah, it was helpful when Noreen explained WAC/WID techniques and then helped them unpack the disciplinary-specific writing process that they had internalized, for in becoming conscious of their own writing processes, they learned to transfer those pedagogies, in an authentic way, to the mathematics writing culture. For Jennifer and Sarah, workshops were a good start, but one-on-one conversations that bridged the disciplinary language gap and examined the authenticity of proposed practices truly brought mathematics and writing pedagogy into congruence. Thus, through Beaufort's high-level questioning focused on the connection between disciplinary goals and writing practices, faculty can develop a deeper understanding of WAC/WID techniques, carefully transform those techniques, and then transfer them to their disciplines.

Works Cited

Bahls, Patrick. "Math and Metaphor: Using Poetry to Teach College Mathematics." *The WAC Journal* 20 (2009): 75-90. Print.

—. *Student Writing in the Quantitative Disciplines*. San Francisco: Jossey Bass, 2012. Print.

Bahls, Patrick, Amy Mecklenburg-Faenger, Meg Scott-Copses, Chris Warnick. "Proofs and Persuasion: A Cross-Disciplinary Analysis of Math Students' Writing." *Across the Disciplines*. Colorado State U, 27 June 2011. Web. 27 September 2012.

Beaufort, Anne. *College Writing and Beyond*. Logan, Utah: Utah State UP, 2007. Print.

Cherkas, Barry M. "A Personal Essay in Math? Getting to Know Your Students." *College Teaching* 40.3 (1992): 83-86. Print.

Epps, Susanna. *Discrete Mathematics with Applications*. Boston: Cengage, 2011. Print.

Estes, Paul. "Writing Across the Mathematics Curriculum." *Writing Across the Curriculum* 1.1 (1989): 10-16. Print.

Fernsten, Linda A. "A Writing Workshop in Mathematics: Community Practice of Content Discourse." *The Mathematics Teacher* 101.4 (2007): 273-78. Print.

Flesher, Tatyana. "Writing to Learn in Mathematics." *The WAC Journal* 14 (2003): 37-48. Print.

Ganguli, Aparna B. "Writing to Learn in Mathematics: Enhancement of Mathematical Understanding." *The AMATYC Review* 16.1 (1994): 45-51. Print.

Gopen, George D., and David A. Smith. "What's an Assignment Like You Doing in a Course Like This? Writing to Learn Mathematics." *The College Mathematics Journal* 21.1 (1990): 2-19. Print.

Grossman, Frances Jo, Brenda Smith, and Cynthia Miller. "Did You Say 'Write' in Mathematics Class?" *Journal of Developmental Education* 17.1 (1993): 2-7. Print.

Halmos, Paul. "The Problem of Learning to Teach." *American Mathematical Monthly* 82 (1975): 466-76. Print.

Knuth, Donald E., Tracy L. Larrabee, and Paul M. Roberts. *Mathematical Writing*. Washington, DC: Mathematical Association of America, 1989. Print.

McCormick, Kelly. "Experiencing the Power of Learning Mathematics through Writing." *IUMPST: The Journal* 4 (2010): 1-8. Print.

Mower, Pat. "Fat Men in Pink Leotards or Students Writing to Learn Algebra." *PRIMUS* 6.4 (1996): 308-24. Print.

Parker, Adam, and Michael Mattison. "By the Numbers." *The WAC Journal* 21 (2010): 37-51. Print.

Russell, David R. *Writing in the Academic Disciplines: A Curricular History*. 2nd ed. Carbondale: Southern Illinois UP, 2002. Print.

Salomon, Gavriel, and David N. Perkins. "Rock Roads to Transfer: Rethinking Mechanisms of a Neglected Phenomenon." *Educational Psychologist* 24.2 (1989): 113-42. Print.

Shepard, Richard G. "Writing for Conceptual Development in Mathematics." *The Journal of Mathematical Behavior* 12.3 (1993): 287-93. Print.

Shibli, Abdullah. "Increasing Learning with Writing in Quantitative and Computer Courses." *College Teaching* 40.4 (1992): 123-27. Print.

Translation, Transformation, and "Taking it Back": Moving between Face-to-Face and Online Writing in the Disciplines

HEIDI SKURAT HARRIS, TAWNYA LUBBES,
NANCY KNOWLES, AND JACOB HARRIS

Faculty teaching face-to-face (F2F) may dread transitioning to online instruction. While scholars have addressed this trepidation for writing faculty (see Warnock; Hewett and Ehmann), this hesitancy can be compounded for faculty across the disciplines who seek to transform both content and writing assignments from the physical to the digital classroom. Online course management systems (CMS) can hinder this task because these systems employ teacher-centered rather than participatory models (Palmquist 406). In addition, developing online courses requires that faculty modify their current pedagogy, often while continuing to juggle their face-to-face courses. Even for seasoned faculty, preparing and delivering an online course can be time-consuming, taking three times as long as a F2F course (Palloff and Pratt 74). In "Online Teaching and Classroom Change: The Trans-classroom Teacher in the Age of the Internet," Susan Lowes calls teachers who are transitioning from F2F to online instruction "trans-classroom teachers," likening them to immigrants "leav[ing] the familiarity of the face-to-face classroom for the uncharted terrain of the online environment, whose constraints and affordances often lead to very different practices." The immigrant metaphor is apt, as instructors transitioning to digital culture must adapt to new problems, behaviors, languages, attitudes, and identities.

Before coming together for a faculty professional development workshop in Summer 2011, each of the authors—faculty members at Eastern Oregon University from English and Writing, Education, and Religious Studies—had faced the challenges of "immigration" alone in our separate disciplines. As we shared our processes of moving our F2F courses online, we found ourselves describing three distinct stages. First, we attempted to "translate" successful F2F strategies into the online environment. In this translation stage, we replicated the F2F activities, assessments, and assignments with little thought about the effect on pedagogy of the change in modality. After initial failed attempts at direct translation, we "transformed" our practice, adjusting our pedagogy to make it more applicable for online delivery. When the CCCC released the 2013 "Position Statement of Principles and Example Effective Practices for Online Writing Instruction (OWI)," we discovered that practices we had arrived at organically through trial and error, alone in our disciplines, were reflected in the experiences of expert online writing instructors across the country.

Even more importantly, perhaps, our conversations about online instruction surfaced a third stage in our pedagogical processes: based on online student success, we found ourselves modifying our F2F practices, "taking back" to the F2F classroom improved activities, scaffolding, and feedback. Thus, transformation of online writing instruction does not represent the conclusion of a neat, linear progression. Instead, regardless of discipline, online delivery can become an integral component of recursive pedagogical practice, in essence, acting as a distancing strategy for thinking through F2F content delivery.

Online Writing Across the Curriculum

Enrollment in online courses has grown steadily in the past ten years. The Babson Group indicates that 32% of college students are enrolled in at least one online course, and online courses were a "critical component" of the long-term strategy at 69% of all higher education institutions in the U.S. (Allen and Seaman 4). However, the implementation of online writing classes often precedes substantive research into sound online writing instruction practices, particularly writing across the curriculum (WAC) online. Research into writing instruction in fully-online classrooms has primarily focused on composition or writing studies classrooms (see the CCCC OWI Bibliography).[1]

Research into WAC work in regard to computer-mediated instruction focuses most often on F2F, networked classrooms or hybrid courses. Donna Reiss, Dickie Self, and Art Young's collection *Electronic Communication Across the Curriculum* (1998) includes guides to implementing computer-mediated instruction across the curriculum, but the only chapter in the book dedicated to online education describes a course that works primarily through email in an era before Facebook, YouTube, or the rise of Google (Chadwick and Dorbolo). More recent work addressing online WAC has focused on assessing online writing (Dean), and even that work has focused on hybrid rather than fully-online courses. A special edition of *Across the Disciplines* titled "Writing Technologies and Writing Across the Curriculum" presumes that online resources and websites primarily serve on-campus or hybrid classes. The most recent survey of WAC programs (2010) gives only brief mention to "electronic technologies" in WAC programs. Chris Thaiss and Tara Porter write, "we can state that the great majority of our respondents did not see the growth of electronic technology per se closely connected to their idea of WAC" (557). In this survey research, "technology" is equated with the implementation of course-management systems and other digital tools in the service of F2F learning. Perhaps the most complete collection to date regarding online WAC is Neff and Whithaus' *Writing*

Across Distances and Disciplines, which acknowledges "many writing and writing-intensive courses delivered from a distance have not reached their potential" (2). In spite of increasing numbers of students taking online classes and higher education's emphasis on increasing online programs, the literature in WAC has not substantially focused on the affordances and constraints of online writing instruction across the curriculum.

While research in computer-mediated or networked classrooms can inform online instruction, effective online classrooms face one challenge not found in either computer-mediated or hybrid classrooms. As Ken Gilliam and Shannon Wooten state:

> The best parts of composition pedagogy are precisely what's missing in most online learning situations. Indeed, the very characteristics of online learning that make it most attractive in university recruitment campaigns—the convenience of learning outside of real time, the ability to work from home or on the go—are the very things that disembody learners, separating them physically and temporally from their professors and classmates. (para. 4)

Online separation from a classroom and disciplinary community may impede the writing process, as students struggle to hone the purpose of their writing with a disembodied audience, to trust their disembodied peers and instructor with authentic communication, and to provide and implement feedback that occurs only in writing, without connection to the spoken words, laughter, and body language that might provide additional guidance and support.

In 2007, the Conference on College Composition and Communication Executive Committee responded to the need for research addressing the teaching of writing in fully online environments by charging the Committee for Best Practices in Online Writing Instruction to develop a position statement, which became the "Position Statement of Principles and Example Effective Practices for Online Writing Instruction" (CCCC OWI; CCCC "Establishing") and represents a starting point for further research into online WAC.

The CCCC OWI Position Statement acknowledges the need for online instruction not only to "translate" but also to "transform" instructional strategies: "Appropriate onsite composition theories, pedagogies, and strategies should be migrated and adapted to the online instructional environment" (Principle 4). F2F techniques based in effective composition theory cannot simply be redeployed for use in the online environment; they must be adapted to suit the modality. For example, Effective Practice 3.5 recommends that "When there is no face-to-face explanatory opportunity and text is the primary means of teaching the writing, [instructors should provide] example strategies for intervening in a clearly written, problem-centered manner" so that online students can better imagine the necessary techniques F2F students acquire through classroom demonstration. Moreover, the modality may present exciting opportunities for alternative methods to deliver some of the best parts of composition pedagogy. For example, Practice 4.2 states, "Teachers [. . .] should employ the interactive potential of digital communications to enable and enact knowledge construction." Because asynchronous online instruction often results in a document trail of interactions in discussion-board posts, wikis, and other forms of shared interaction, the potential exists for students not only to enact knowledge construction but also to study, use, and value that interaction. Thus, while research on computer-mediated and hybrid WAC classes might inform our work, research into effective pedagogy in fully-online WAC courses, guided by the CCCC OWI Position Statement, will be vital as twenty-first century classrooms continue to move into cyberspace. While the Position Statement arises from research in and practitioners from the field of writing studies, these principles can guide online writing instruction across disciplines, as our pedagogical transformations indicate.

Online Writing-in-the-Disciplines at Eastern Oregon University

Our transformative practice, as well as our participation in summer institute training in August 2011, centers on our university mission to "connect the rural regions of Oregon to a wider world" (Eastern Oregon University, "Mission and Values Statement"). Eastern Oregon University (EOU) is a small, liberal-arts university located in La Grande, Oregon. As of winter quarter 2014, EOU enrolled 3,731 students (FTE=2,471), with just under half of those students fully online (FTE=1,186). In addition to on-campus courses at our main campus in La Grande and online courses, EOU has sixteen regional centers throughout the state of Oregon. These regional centers serve an additional 657 students (FTE=231) in over 45 Oregon counties (EOU, "Institutional Research"). Because Oregon is largely rural, distance education courses, initially correspondence courses and later online and on-site courses have been a substantial component of EOU for over thirty years. EOU currently offers ten fully online four-year bachelor's degrees as well as eighteen fully online minors.

To promote strong writing skill in this geographically dispersed population, EOU has instituted the University Writing Requirement (UWR). The UWR "requires that students receive attention to writing throughout their studies and that students demonstrate their mastery of discipline-specific writing" (EOU, "University Writing Requirement"). To this end, students are required to take the first-year composition course (WR 121: Expository Writing), one lower-level UWR course, and two-upper division UWR courses as specified by their major. UWR course outcomes include a minimum number of written words (both in draft and polished form), attention to discipline-specific conventions, multiple drafts, integration of sources relevant to their discipline and cited appropriately, and attention to peer review and feedback from the instructor at multiple stages of the drafting process.

In spite of EOU's long history with online education and significant focus on writing across the curriculum, faculty professional development in technology for writing purposes has been limited. EOU supports a robust National Writing Project site, but university faculty wanted additional training in instructional technologies. In Summer 2011, a group of faculty came together for the first Summer Institute for Instructional Technology (SIIT), a two-week workshop that investigated best practices in online teaching and learning co-coordinated by Heidi Skurat Harris and Steve Clements. Sixteen participants from across the university participated in the inaugural institute, which centered on California State University-Chico's Rubric for Online Instruction's six components of effective online instruction (see http://www.csuchico.edu/celt/roi/ for more information about the rubric).

As three of these participants—Nancy Knowles (English and Writing), Tawnya Lubbes (Education), and Jacob Harris (Religious Studies)—shared their techniques for effective online instruction, they discovered that effective writing instruction posed some particular challenges in their online classes: promoting student engagement and interaction, helping students navigate the overwhelming amount of reading and writing in the online classroom, and scaffolding and sequencing course activities to help online students complete longer writing assignments effectively.

Although we taught in different content areas at Eastern Oregon University, we also found striking similarities in our transitions between the F2F and online environments. First, we needed to facilitate online learning more intentionally than F2F learning; interacting with students, "being present" in the class, was key to success. This finding is consistent with CCCC OWI Position Statement Effective Practice 3.10, which argues, "Teachers should moderate online class discussions to develop a collaborative OWC and to ensure participation of all students, the free and productive exchange of ideas, and a constant habit of written expression with a genuine audience." Second, multimedia and interactive resources frequently and somewhat counter-intuitively led to better writing. This discovery is consistent with the CCCC OWI Position Statement Effective Practice 3.2, that argues for blending "different and redundant modalities." We discovered that writing *more effectively*, not *more frequently*, achieved University Writing Requirement outcomes. Third, in the online medium, we needed to replace classroom dialogue with shorter written assignments, scaffold larger assignments more clearly, and sequence activities more effectively. This discovery is consistent with CCCC OWI Position Statement Effective Practice 4.1: "When migrating from onsite modalities to the online environment, teachers should break their assignments, exercises, and activities into smaller units to increase opportunities for interaction between teacher and student and among students using both asynchronous and synchronous modalities." In turn, success with these transformations of our writing pedagogy encouraged us to revisit the effectiveness of our F2F classroom practices and use the distance provided by the online modality to realize that F2F students also benefit from the strategies developed for the online environment.

Translation: Moving Writing Instruction Online

The three instructors who participated in the SIIT 2011, Nancy Knowles (English and Writing), Tawnya Lubbes (Education), and Jacob Harris (Religious Studies) all were tasked with moving writing instruction in their disciplines (practiced not in computer-mediated classrooms or even necessarily in classrooms with robust wireless access) to online modalities. In doing so, they faced challenges in helping students access course content and materials and using those materials effectively. According to Elizabeth Barkley, Professor of Music at Foothill College and author of *Student Engagement Techniques: A Handbook for College Faculty*, only 4% of learners prefer reading as a means of processing information compared to 18% discussion, 27% hands-on learning, and 31% teaching others (139). These figures indicate that access as a component of course delivery is not just a matter of difficulty for those outside the institution, those with hardware limitations, or those with disabilities (Porter 215-16); access is a vital component of the online experience for students attempting to join academic conversations, "those [not] already in the know," (Taylor 133), as the print or text-based modes of interaction may render some conversations inaccessible for particular students.

Nancy: Reading and Writing as a Barrier to Reading and Writing Online

When Nancy Knowles, Professor of English and Writing, began teaching literature and technical writing online in 2003, her primary strategy to teach reading and writing was through reading and writing. She simply translated process-writing strategies into the online environment. The online environment revealed limitations of the process approach: at the time, online students had almost no other option for interaction with teachers and peers aside from reading and writing, modes that often failed to replicate the valuable interpersonal collaboration common to the F2F classroom.

Transitioning between F2F and online instruction highlighted problems associated with unexamined emphasis on written text as a means to teach writing and content. Although writing-immersed pedagogy benefits students by encouraging development of literacy skills (Courage 170; Warnock xi), written text may not always be the best access point for students to engage with literate tasks, particularly in an online environment often dominated by written text and particularly for first-year and struggling students for whom reading and writing represent significant challenges. Struggling students manifested a host of problematic behaviors, the most serious of which was simple absence from the online environment. Bombarded with a text-based welcome page, a written syllabus, a dense print textbook or poetry anthology, a bewildering set of folders filled with written lectures and assignment instructions, a discussion board filled with other students apparently capably and confidently posting writing, and later a set of text-based instructor emails asking whether they needed assistance, the path of least resistance was to avoid interaction. Struggling students who attempted to engage did their best to deliver on expectations, producing "safe" posts either vague enough to try to hide confusion or mimicking or outright copying the seemingly successful posts of other students. If they survived the instructor (written) encouragement to improve, they produced mechanical kinds of writing that indicated an ongoing perception of coursework as busywork, not as access to personally enlightening material or professionally beneficial skills. In the online section of WR 320: Technical Writing in Summer 2006, for example, the class average was 67%, which indicates the course could have better served struggling students.

Jacob: Too Much Writing Online

Similar to Nancy's text-based approach to enter into reading and writing, Jacob Harris, Instructor in Religious Studies, discovered that F2F discussion did not translate directly into written discussion in his introduction to religion and more advanced religious studies courses. When Jacob first started teaching online in 2006, his experience teaching in the F2F classroom involved his work as a graduate teaching assistant, where senior faculty mentors encouraged long faculty lectures supplemented by shorter discussion groups. When he translated this method to online classes, he found himself telling students to "read the textbook" to replace the lectures and then assigning two discussion questions or prompts each week with two required classmate responses for each question. This method closely replicated the "lecture and discuss" methods from his large F2F religious studies courses.

In addition to replicating this lecture-and-discuss pedagogy, Jacob assumed that students would improve their writing in the discussion forums and in longer written assignments by writing more frequently. However, Jacob found that students, who might have willingly referenced print sources in a F2F classroom, struggled to synthesize such sources in their discussion board posts. Students spent so much time writing weekly discussion posts (the equivalent of two full essays per week) and responding to classmates that they were completing the bare minimum to get by, the quality was rushed and superficial, and they failed to truly engage in discussions with each other. Moreover, because of the massive amount of student writing, Jacob found himself struggling to engage with students on discussion boards to model discussion and highlight relevant course concepts. Writing on discussion boards, in addition to content-writing (such as the twice per term New Religious Experience essays) and readings from the textbook and supplemental readings, meant an overwhelming reading and writing load for students and himself. As a result, his attrition rates hovered around 50% and additional students simply "disappeared" from the class even while still enrolled.

Tawnya: Need for Scaffolding Online

Tawnya Lubbes, Assistant Professor of Education, was asked in 2009 to teach a special online section of her Language and Cognition course for a small group of students. This was her first experience with teaching the writing process online. Without realizing the need to transform her F2F course for online delivery, she included PowerPoint presentations to replicate F2F instruction time and discussion boards to replicate in-class discussion. All other course assignments remained as presented F2F, which included weekly reading response guides, drafts of writing assignments, and written reflections. The overarching activity in the course was an in-depth case study of a bilingual informant, including a "thick description" (see Geertz) and an analysis of theoretically salient issues in terms of language acquisition. This activity demanded synthesis, application and evaluative cognitive thinking skills. Students also needed background in the foundations of bilingual education and bilingualism, linguistic analysis, and common miscues of second language learning, and they needed to write analytically using scholarly tone and APA formatting.

To complete this activity in the F2F course, Tawnya placed students into literature and peer editing groups. Students read and revised their writing through a multi-step process, submitting their writing in segments and receiving ample feedback to build toward their final drafts. Tawnya provided F2F students examples of previous studies and guided them through the writing process (again reinforcing the need for recursive feedback indicated in OWI Effective Practice 4.1).

Online, Tawnya simply translated elements of the course without transforming them, without scaffolding the information and writing process for the students. She provided PowerPoint presentations without narratives or opportunities for interaction. Discussion questions related to the readings required limited student dialogue. Tawnya encouraged students to complete peer editing or use the Writing Center, but neither activity was required. Because Tawnya did not have time to gather permission from former students to scan and post copies online, examples of the case study were not provided. While she presented a variety of online resources in the CMS, students received little direction for using the resources. While Tawnya identified weekly deadlines, she allowed multiple drafts, even if significantly late. This leniency meant that, rather than moving forward, students spent time rewriting previous work and falling further behind. All in all, the online class produced lower quality case studies than the F2F class. In the F2F class the course average was an 82%, while the online course students averaged 76%. In particular, the online students failed to build upon the background knowledge gained through course readings by connecting the sections of the case study with the chapters from the course text.

While navigating their online writing courses, all three experienced F2F instructors struggled with communicating writing assignments, modeling academic discourse, and giving students the guidance that they needed to complete complex projects and integrate source materials. In the online environment, as Gilliam and Wooten note, students lacked access to the structures that made classroom learning powerful and effective: visual and aural cues, the presence of a reflective practitioner who could informally assess success from moment to moment and adjust delivery to meet student needs, and the physical reality of a community of learners whose presence modeled strategies, provided emotional support, and encouraged questions and deeper thought. Online environments replacing the dynamic of F2F classrooms with inert and overwhelming materials proved to struggling students that college-level work was beyond their capacities.

Transformation: From Transmission to Engagement

As the instructors faced their failures in their online courses, they each sought to overhaul their online classes in order to more effectively meet the needs of diverse learners who were "separated physically and temporally from their classmates," (Gilliam and Wooten) while struggling to synthesize and integrate new, affectively and cognitively challenging content into their writing.

Nancy: Going Native

In 2009, Nancy began to "go native" (Taylor 139)—that is, to adapt instructional strategies to the students served. To use Porter's words, online access "means starting the writing [or course development] process from audience and working backward to made object [or online course]" (216; see also Savenye, Olina, and Niemczyk). In moving between F2F and online instruction, Nancy discovered multimedia and multi-modal projects as "appropriate strategies" not only "adapted to the online instructional environment," per Practice 4 (CCCC OWI), but also helping in enhancing access to literate learning in all classes.

To serve online students needing access to literate discourse, Nancy broadened the strategies by which she invited student response. At first, she envisioned the daunting task of meeting student needs by knowing them well enough to match their preferences to particular assignments and worried over the fact that learners should also be encouraged to stretch beyond their preferences. But soon, she realized that, as Enujoo Oh and Doohun Lim, researchers in instructional technology at the University of Tennessee, conclude, attempting to match learners to particular assignments was less important than simply providing a variety of access points. Rather than completing one assignment in lockstep with peers, students benefit by options whereby they can self-select the best means to demonstrate skills and knowledge. Nancy's online students responded well to photographing art, clustering, and mapping; using video to capture performances (such as one memorable Bollywood dance routine); and using blogs for interactive public dialogue to stimulate engagement. Creative writing also enhanced emotional and aesthetic engagement with academic writing. Blending media and genres acknowledges that "writing is Technicolor, oral, and thoroughly integrated with visual and audio displays," representing a "secondary literacy" (Diogenes and Lunsford 142), a literacy particularly appropriate to students already learning in an online environment. Using both text and non-text methods of reaching out to students, allowing students to interact visually and aurally through multimedia, opened avenues to writing. Reading and writing operated not as the sole means of communication but as a natural progression from other activities. As a result, the atmosphere and quality of work in Nancy's online courses changed. Students spent time on the discussion board laughing and commiserating over one another's posts, building a classroom community for all participants, not just those confident with text-based forms of communication. Writing produced in these courses became more engaged, more a combination of academic skill and personal interests and therefore more valuable to the students themselves, which ramped up the quality. As an index of the change, the course average for online students enrolled in ENGL 221: Sophomore Seminar in Winter 2013 surpassed that of the on-campus section (85% to 72%).

Jacob: Fewer, Better Written Assignments

To transform his online courses and to help students integrate affectively and cognitively difficult source material in discussion board posts and writing assignments, Jacob scaled back the number of required discussion board postings from two posts every week to one post every two weeks. In a 2007 study, Wang and Woo found that online students have more time to "think, clarify, and respond" to their classmates and can rely more heavily on using sources and other materials to support themselves than they can in F2F discussions (281), but because of the more time-consuming nature of the written discussion, the online discussion time-frame needed to be much longer (284). Thus, online discussions can help students improve their synthesis and research skills but only when students are not overwhelmed with a multitude of text- or print-based reading and writing activities. The "less is more" philosophy also applies to instructor texts where concision aids in avoiding confusion (Ragain and White 406).

In alternating activity weeks, Jacob supplemented text-based sources with videos and audio recordings in which adherents of a variety of religions discussed their experiences in those religious traditions, which aligns with CCCC OWI Effective Practice 3.2 "Text-based instruction should be supplemented with oral and/or video instruction in keeping with the need for presenting instruction in different and redundant modalities." In discussion boards, students synthesized concepts from the textbook with the experiences of those who practiced the religions they were studying and theories posed by religious studies scholars. Just as Nancy incorporated audio, video, and kinesthetic activities as a way of differentiating instruction to make literate conversations accessible, Jacob incorporated these tools as an entrance to difficult scholarly discussions about the secular, academic study of religion.

Besides requiring fewer posts, Jacob clarified the requirements for discussion boards and encouraged students to include their own experiences as well as synthesizing sources. George Collison, Bonnie Elbaum, Sarah Haavind, and Robert Tinker, authors of *Facilitating Online Learning: Effective Strategies for Moderators*, reinforce these practices, suggesting that a healthy online discussion has clearly defined expectations and reminders of those expectations in the directions for each board (78-80). They further advise that discussion boards encourage deep dialogue where participants think critically about content (140). After the changes to the discussion board criteria, students in Jacob's religious studies classes spent more time in deep dialogue with their classmates. And, just as Warnock recommends (79), this deep dialogue constituted a significant portion (30%) of the course grade. In addition to dialogue in discussion boards, students interacted with each other to complete group projects in all of his online classes, further integrating course concepts and personal experiences while interacting with each other.

During his discussions with students, Jacob also transformed the focus of his feedback from end-of-discussion summative assessments to formative assessment. Instead of waiting until the end of the week to identify an excellent comment or post, fewer discussion boards meant that Jacob had more time to participate during class discussion, pointing out excellent student input in the flow of discussion. This practice conforms to OWI Effective Practice 3.5 regarding instructors' role in guiding improvement: "When there is no face-to-face explanatory opportunity and text is the primary means of teaching the writing, example strategies for intervening in a clearly written, problem-centered manner include … modeling by writing at the level that is being required of the student and providing doable tasks with instructions" (CCCC OWI).

In addition to including discussion board rubrics, samples of both adequate and insufficient posts, and discussion of the problems with insufficient posts, Jacob supported student success by modeling the discourse he asked of students. He followed his own rules, incorporating outside sources, passages of the textbook, and authentic leading questions. As a result of this guidance, Jacob's students not only synthesized sources more clearly in discussion board posts, but they also transferred those writing skills to longer written texts, such as the New Religious Experience assignment where students analyze an unfamiliar religious ritual. In addition, student attrition rates dropped to around 30% and those students enrolled in the course were more likely to complete more of the assignments and successfully complete the class.

Tawnya: Scaffolding Online Student Work

Transitioning between F2F and online instruction not only emphasized the need for Tawnya to improve student interaction and incorporate multimedia elements to support print-based materials but also revealed the need to scaffold and sequence course assignments so that online students could complete tasks without synchronous or real-time direction from faculty. OWI **Effective Practice 4.1 identifies the need for instructors to** "break their assignments, exercises, and activities into smaller units to increase opportunities for interaction between teacher and student and among students using both asynchronous and synchronous modalities" (CCCC OWI). In addition to online scaffolding, Tawnya incorporated peer review in online classes. Miky Ronan and Dorothy Langley, authors of "Scaffolding Complex Tasks by Open Online Submission: Emerging Patterns and Profiles," incorporate student review and commentary in their "open online submission," where students submit parts of writing at various stages for other students and faculty to review. This process not only assists students in understanding the task but also permits instructors to identify communication problems and intervene (58). Because peer review requires risk-taking in sharing documents, it has the potential to build trust necessary to form a learning community comprised of multiple and valued perspectives in the manner that F2F courses do.

After evaluating the pitfalls of simply translating the course from F2F to online, Tawnya modified the course to integrate all four of the scaffolding strategies that Michael Hannafin, Susan Land and Kevin Oliver's "Open Learning Environments: Foundations, Methods, and Models" identifies: 1) procedural scaffolds to help give and clarify directions, 2) conceptual scaffolds that guide learners into working through multiple concepts, 3) metacognitive scaffolds that prompt students to look at the subject from multiple perspectives, and 4) strategic scaffolds, including alternative approaches to planning and application processes.

Procedural scaffolds included the reorganization of the course structure. Outside resources appeared in units that corresponded with each section of the case study. The revised course also scheduled regular due dates in order to keep the students on track. In creating conceptual scaffolds, she realigned textbook chapters to match the specific sections of the case study as students completed them. Metacognitive and strategic scaffolds included collaborative learning groups and the requirement that students submit reviews of work and summaries of the students' editing group progress. Some of this peer interaction occurred within the Blackboard™ CMS in order to allow Tawnya to facilitate and monitor the progress, providing the instructor intervention and support that Carla Garnam and Robert Kaleta, published in *Teaching with Technology Today,* deem necessary to help students manage their time and expectations. In addition, she designed discussion board prompts to ask higher-order questions (see Collison et al. and Warnock) and to assist students in developing inquiry methods to gather information for their case studies. Tawnya also modified PowerPoint™ presentations to include instructor notes and summaries. In presenting the case study assignment, she worked from whole to part and part to whole, providing the big picture of the case study (including individual case studies completed by previous students) and then breaking that picture down into units that integrated all four scaffolding strategies.

As a result of her efforts, students in the second online version of the course produced some of the best quality case studies Tawnya had ever seen, all while meeting the course objectives. Students in this course moved from the previous 76% average to an 89% average in the transformed course section. Positive written and verbal feedback from the students confirmed success. One student stated: "I learned a lot of new stuff and it was good to finally be able to use everything we have learned. I am so glad we had sections of our case study due throughout the term." Another student advised: "the breaking down of the final paper into sections was particularly helpful for successfully completing the course." Further, Tawnya was able to share her course redesign with her colleagues who taught the same course in online and hybrid formats.

By transforming their instruction to better support online learners, Nancy, Jacob, and Tawnya achieved noticeable improvements in students' academic performance. The application of multi-media and multimodal projects and a broadening of strategies and access points in their courses allowed for learners to meet their course objectives without the struggle in communicating via one-dimensional procedural writing. Scaffolding, clear guiding directions, increased frequency of interactions, and instructional design that was less text-driven and more focused on visuals, including video and audio recordings, greatly contributed to the successes the instructors observed in their courses. The three also recognized that specific grading criteria with frequent feedback mechanisms assisted the students in understanding and meeting the course requirements. Through these strategies, online students became more engaged with course materials and activities and more successful in demonstrating acquired knowledge and skills.

Taking It Back: Energizing the Face-to-Face Classroom with Online Strategies

While the CCCC OWI Position Statement addresses the need to transform pedagogy when moving from the F2F to the online environment, it doesn't address the impact of online instruction on F2F instruction. As increasing numbers of recursive practitioners teach in both modalities, they may find the online teaching experience informing their F2F practice. Once Nancy, Jacob, and Tawnya saw student improvement in their online courses, they began to take back lessons from those courses to their F2F classes.

Nancy and Jacob: More Productive Use of Multimedia and F2F Class Time

Expanding Nancy's repertoire of online delivery methods has reinforced the necessity of access in the F2F setting. In online teaching, "seat time" is replaced by time engaged in meaningful course activities. This experience helped Nancy re-envision her use of F2F class time as devoted to productive hands-on work. In writing classes, rather than attempting to cover one element of writing everyone in the class needs to practice (which is not possible), Nancy usually spends the beginning of the week in interactive activities and devotes the end of the week to writing time, coaching, and response to drafts—freeing students to work individually or in small groups on the aspect of writing that most needs their attention. Nancy also finds technology playing an increased role in her F2F classroom, as Blackboard becomes a repository for drafts and a place for peer review.

Jacob's F2F practice now benefits from his online use of multimedia and discussion strategies. Students in his F2F Introduction to Religion course, for example, create their own religion as a final synthesis activity, giving F2F presentations and also compiling supplementary online resources. Modeling academic discourse and discussion has become the focus of Jacob's classes. Unlike the lecture courses Jacob delivered as a graduate student, he now asks students to give mini-presentations on course material, complete daily "check-in" writing, and he provides guidance and feedback in active discussion with the students. CCCC OWI Effective Practice 3.10, which states that "Teachers should moderate online class discussions to develop a collaborative OWC and to ensure participation of all students, the free and productive exchange of ideas, and a constant habit of written expression with a genuine audience" not only transformed his online pedagogy but his F2F pedagogy as well, helping him to overcome the restrictive "lecture and discuss" methods of his graduate training.

Jacob's and Nancy's transitions between F2F and online instruction also demonstrate that multimedia and active learning facilitate writing. Both classrooms provide students new means of synthesizing difficult course content thorough hands-on and collaborative activities. Writing resulted from these practices more organically, becoming a part of the course as a result of, and in some cases in response to, the visual, auditory, and kinesthetic experiences students encountered in their classes.

In addition, both Nancy and Jacob addressed the affective element of transitioning from personal to scholarly writing. For Nancy, multimedia and active learning helped students overcome anxieties associated with writing by connecting with topics, developing a deep reservoir of ideas, and even producing outstanding personal writing before turning to academic writing, armed with the interest, ideas, and sentences. In Jacob's religion courses, he struggled with ardent believers' affective responses to the secular academic study of religion, encountering perspectives through a non-faith-based lens as they studied as "critics not caretakers" (McCutcheon). The use of multimedia in both F2F and online classes allowed students to witness adherents of various faiths discuss their beliefs and helped students stimulate various parts of the brain, enhancing the creation of new neural networks to process difficult scholarly criticism (Costa and Nuhfer) and moving from defenses of their own faith practices into open consideration of the practices of other faiths, moving them effectively toward higher affective domain competencies.

Tawnya: Improved F2F Scaffolding

Because of the success of the revised online course, Tawnya integrated the new strategies of scaffolding into the F2F classroom. She provided an overview of the case study at the beginning of the course and then broke the instruction and course readings down into units. Each unit then corresponded to a section of the paper that the students would write and revise, thus providing the necessary references and support for each section. Additionally, Tawnya redesigned the peer editing groups to employ a writer's workshop format where each individual was responsible for a component of the editing process each week (see Armstrong and Paulson). During the peer review process, she also required regular progress reports. Tawnya, like Nancy and Jacob, used the online platform as a place to store unit resources, rubrics and other course documents for the F2F classroom. Finally, the Blackboard Grade Center™ was integrated into the F2F class in order to track progress. These modifications of the F2F class improved student writing quality and consistency in meeting course outcomes. Most importantly, just as Armstrong and Paulson predicted,

Tawnya found the course easier to deliver, and students provided positive feedback about the learning process.

As increasing numbers of faculty members across disciplines—like Nancy, Jacob, and Tawnya—teach in both the F2F and online environments, we can expect increased reflections on the intersections between teaching modalities. It seems obvious that the online classroom would translate strategies from the F2F classroom into the online environment because the F2F classroom came first. In addition, as the CCCC OWI Position Statement and this research indicate, faculty members must not only translate but transform those strategies to meet the needs of online learners. Perhaps even more interesting is the swirling occurring not only among students enrolling in courses employing a variety of modalities but also among faculty members teaching a wide range of technology-enhanced courses, from traditional F2F courses with a CMS repository of materials to courses housed fully online in the CMS environment. As faculty members swirl, their professional development will should naturally take lessons learned in the online modality back to the F2F classroom, and those lessons may in turn transform the F2F classroom. Based on the experiences of Nancy, Jacob, and Tawnya, the movement from online to F2F modalities suggests particular benefits to swirling: because the online environment distances faculty members from the culture of their F2F classrooms, teaching online can help them better perceive the quality of F2F delivery. In addition, online instruction demands more explicit scaffolding simply because instructors are not physically present to ad-lib instruction. Thus, online instruction becomes a "sandbox" for imagining explicit media, scaffolding, and use of class time that might also enhance F2F instruction.

Translation, Transformation, Taking It Back: Concluding Thoughts

With the rise in popularity of online courses, many universities are increasing their online or hybrid offerings to "keep up with the continuing population growth and demands for lifelong learning" (Bleed qtd. in Young A34). Increased demand for online courses obligates faculty to transform their F2F strategies for the electronic environment so that all students can access learning, but increased online teaching loads also provide a unique opportunity as part of reflective practice to take newly re-imagined strategies back to the F2F classroom. Our individual experiences, combined with insights from the CCCC OWI Position Statement of Principles and Example Effective Practices for Online Writing Instruction, provide a starting point for faculty seeking to undergo similar transformational practices and for further research into the effectiveness of these particular practices in relation to WAC anywhere on the F2F-online spectrum. Key conclusions include the following principles.

Students need the opportunity to learn from a variety of media (*Effective Practice* 3.2).

Because communication in online courses still relies mainly on writing, as Nancy's and Jacob's experiences indicate, online students need fewer, better written assignments, combined with multimedia texts and the chance to demonstrate learning through multimedia options. Similarly, when we take this learning from the online "sandbox" back to the F2F classroom, we must recognize that while F2F students have more opportunities for interpersonal interaction in the classroom, they, too, benefit from multimedia pathways to writing and opportunities to "write" using multimedia tools. Additional research on the effectiveness of using multi-modal elements should be conducted to understand the specific relationships between multimodal instruction and increased writing competencies across the curriculum.

Students need models and scaffolding (*Effective Practice* 3.5 and 4.1).

Because online students lack F2F opportunities to hear instructors discuss writing assignments and answer questions about them and because putting questions into writing requires more student effort, online students need models and explanatory activities—such as those outlined in Effective Practice 3.5, including instructions and questions, and those provided by Michael Hannafin, Susan Land and Kevin Oliver—to better comprehend assignments and difficult concepts. For example, when Tawnya needed students to incorporate an understanding of bilingualism, linguistic analysis, and second language miscues into their case studies, including sequenced examples and scaffolding, instruction helped students work through complex content-area synthesis and produce better writing. When Jacob needed to help his students move beyond lower-order affective reactions and more complex interactions with religious studies theory, he modeled the discourse he expected his students to achieve. As Effective Practice 4.1 indicates, scaffolding and modeling not only build student understanding but also enhance interactions among teacher and students. As students receive more frequent peer and instructor feedback on smaller assignments, they experience less isolation and more engagement. While F2F students receive ongoing feedback from their peers and instructor through classroom interaction, they also find models and scaffolding activities beneficial. In this way, using online instruction as a "sandbox" can assist reflective practitioners in developing more precise supports to make learning accessible for all students. Additional research in this area could include examining the relationship between various types of scaffolding and modeling practices and students' abilities to enter academic discourse communities.

> Students need faculty presence and disciplinary community (*Effective Practice* 3.10 and 4.2).

In the process of better serving online students, Nancy, Jacob, and Tawnya became more active on the discussion board. Tawnya and Jacob, in particular, found themselves using discussion boards for more in-depth student engagement as well as to demonstrate student mastery of course concepts. As Effective Practice 3.10 observes, instructor collaboration with students in discussion boards "ensure[s] participation of all students, the free and productive exchange of ideas, and a constant habit of written expression with a genuine audience." Providing interactive spaces for students helped to mitigate some of the isolation issues online students experience in being distant both spatially and temporally from each other and from the instructor. Even in the F2F environment, students need to experience faculty members as present, as collaborators in a discourse community that includes students. After all, the heart of successful WAC efforts is helping students develop new knowledge bases constructively. Using the online "sandbox" to explore course dialogue as disciplinary community-building encourages F2F faculty members to transform "seat time," as all three faculty members did, into opportunities for the active practice of knowledge construction, building the discourse communities necessary to support students in navigating the unfamiliar terrain of new texts, research methods and theories in our disciplines. While a number of studies across the disciplines have examined effective practices in using discussion boards, among other collaborative strategies, more work needs to be done with the relationship between faculty interaction and student engagement in these online spaces, and in building disciplinary discourse communities through classroom dialogue.

The remarkable consistency across the teaching practice of the faculty authors involved in this project, who have a total of thirty years of combined online teaching experience, reflects the need for all faculty to pause and consider the moves they make while immigrating from the "home country" of the F2F classroom into foreign territory of online education and also when returning home, equipped with new perspectives. And as we transform our courses, we transform ourselves as teachers, and ultimately, as lifelong learners.

Notes

1. Some research from outside the field of rhetoric and composition has also been conducted and upholds the need for engagement in WAC courses, indicating that engaged students who participated in discussion boards and received feedback from the instructor were more likely to be successful in classes (Defazio, Jones, Tennant, and Hook).

Works Cited

Allen, Elaine I. and Jeff Seaman. "Changing Course: Ten Years of Tracking Online Education in the United States." Babson Survey Research Group. 2013. Web. 21 Oct. 2014.

Armstrong, Sonya and Eric Paulson. "Whither Peer Review? Terminology Matters for the Writing Classroom." *Teaching English at the Two Year College* 35.4 (2008): 398-407. Print.

Barkley, Elizabeth F. *Student Engagement Techniques: A Handbook for College Faculty.* San Francisco: Jossey-Bass, 2009. Print.

California State University-Chico (CSU-Chico). "What Does a High-Quality Online Course Look Like?" California State University-Chico Rubric for Online Instruction. n.d. Web. 10 February 2012.

Chadwick, Scott and Jon Dorbolo. "Inter-Quest: Designing a Communication-Intensive Web-Based Course." In Reiss, Selfe, and Young. 118-28.

Collison, George, Bonnie Elbaum, Sarah Haavind, and Robert Tinker. *Facilitating Online Learning: Effective Strategies for Moderators.* Madison, WI: Atwood Publishing 2000. Print.

Conference on College Composition and Communication (CCCC). "Establishing a Statement of Principles for Online Writing Instruction (OWI)." 9 April 2013. Web. 20 April 2014.

—. "A Position Statement of Principles and Example Effective Practices for Online Writing Instruction." 13 November 2013. Web. 21 Oct. 2014.

Costa, Maria and Ed Nuhfer. "Psychomotor Domain: How We Learn Physical Skills Can Teach Us Something." California State University-Los Angeles and California State University-Channel Islands. 10 February 2012. Web. 21 Oct. 2014.

Courage, Richard. "Asynchronicity: Delivering Composition and Literature in the Cyberclassroom." Yancey 168-82.

Dean, Christopher. "Developing and Assessing an Online Research Course." *Across the Disciplines* 6. 19 Jan. 2009. Web. 21 Oct. 2014.

Defazio, Joseph, Josette Jones, Felisa Tennant, and Sarah Anne Hook. "Academic Literacy: The Importance and Impact of Writing Across the Curriculum—A Case Study." *Journal of the Scholarship of Teaching and Learning* 10.2 (June 2010): 34-47. Print.

Diogenes, Marvin, and Andrea A. Lunsford. "Toward Delivering New Definitions of Writing." Yancey 141-54.

—. "Institutional Research." N.d. Web. 29 Jan. 2014.

—. "Mission and Values Statement." Office of the President. February 3, 2004. Web.

—. "University Writing Requirement." N.d. Web.

Garnam, Carla and Robert Kaleta. "Introduction to Hybrid Courses." *Teaching with Technology Today* 8.6 (2002). 10 February 2012. Web.

Geertz, Clifford. *The Interpretation of Cultures.* New York: Basic Books Publishing, 2000. Print.

Gibson, Keith and Beth Hewett. "Annotated Bibliography: CCCC Committee on Best Practices in Online Writing Instruction." N.d. Web.

Gilliam, Ken and Shannon Wooten. "Re-embodying Online Composition: Ecologies of Writing in Unreal Time and Space." *Computers and Composition Online*. Spring 2014. Web.

Hannafin, Michael, Susan Land and Kevin Oliver. "Open Learning Environments: Foundations, Methods, and Models." *Instructional Design Theories and Models: A New Paradigm of Instructional Theory*. Ed. C. M. Reigeluth. vol. II. Mahwah, NJ: Erlbaum, 1999. 115-140. Print.

Hewett, Beth and Christa Ehmann. *Preparing Educators for Online Writing Instruction: Principles and Processes*. Urbana: NCTE, 2004. Print.

Hewett, Beth. *The Online Writing Conference*. Heineman: Portsmouth, NH, 2011.

Lowes, Susan. "Online Teaching and Classroom Change: The Trans-classroom Teacher in the Age of the Internet." *Innovate* 4.3: (2008). 10 February 2012. Web.

Lundsford, Karen J. ed. "Writing Technologies and Writing Across the Disciplines: Current Lessons and Future Trends." *Across the Disciplines*. January 19, 2009. Web.

McCutcheon, Russell T. *Critics not Caretakers: Redescribing the Public Study of Religion*. Albany: SUNY University Press, 2001. Print.

Neff, Joyce Magnotto, and Carl Whithaus. *Writing Across Distances and Disciplines: Research and Pedagogy in Distributed Learning*. New York: Lawrence Erlbaum, 2008.

Oh, Eunjoo, and Doohun Lim. "Cross Relationships between Cognitive Styles and Learner Variables in Online Learning Environment." *Journal of Interactive Online Learning* 4.1 (Summer 2005): 53-66.

Palmquist, Michael. "A Brief History of Computer-Support for Writing Centers and Writing-Across-the Curriculum Programs." *Computers and Composition* 20.4 (2003): 395-413. 4 June 2012. Web.

Palloff, Rena, and Keith Pratt. *Building Online Learning Communities*. San Francisco: Jossey-Bass, 2007. Print.

Porter, James E. "Recovering Delivery for Digital Rhetoric." *Computers & Composition* 26.4 (2009): 207-224. *Academic Search Premier*. 7 June 2012. Web.

Ragan, Tillman J., and Patricia R. White. "What We Have Here Is a Failure to Communicate: The Criticality of Writing in Online Instruction." *Computers and Composition* 18 (2001): 399-409. Print.

Reiss, Donna, Dickie Selfe, and Art Young. *Electronic Communication Across the Curriculum*. WAC Clearinghouse. Spring 1998. Web.

Ronan, Miky, and Dorothy Langley. "Scaffolding Complex Tasks by Open Online Submission: Emerging Patterns and Profiles." *Journal of Asynchronous Learning Networks* 8:4 (2004). 39-61. 18 June 2012. Web.

Savenye, Wilhelmina C., Zane Olina, and Mary Niemczyk. "So You Are Going to Be an Online Writing Instructor: Issues in Designing, Developing, and Delivering an Online Course." *Computers and Composition* 18.4 (2001): 371-85. *ERIC*. 7 June 2012. Web.

Thaiss, Chris, and Tara Porter. " The State of WAC/WID in 2010: Methods and Results of the U.S. Survey of the International WAC/WID Mapping Project." *College Composition and Communication* 61.3 (February 2010). 534-570. Print.

Taylor, Todd. "Design, Delivery, and Narcolepsy." Yancey 127-40.

Wang, Qiyun, and Huay Lit Woo. "Systematic Planning for ICT Integration in Topic Learning." *Educational Technology & Society* 10.1 (2007): 148-156. Web.

Warnock, Scott. *Teaching Writing Online*. Urbana: NCTE, 2009. Print.

Yancey, Kathleen Blake, ed. *Delivering College Composition: The Fifth Canon*. Poetsmouth, NH: Boynton/Cook, 2006. Print.

Young, Jeffrey. "'Hybrid' teaching seeks to end the divide between traditional and online instruction." *The Chronicle of Higher Education* 48.28 (2002): A33-34. 10 February 2012. Web.

Stephen Wilhoit:
A Stealth WAC Practitioner

CAROL RUTZ

When I asked Steve Wilhoit of the University of Dayton whether I could interview him for this series in *The WAC Journal*, his response was characteristic: "Did you send your request to the right guy?" Despite regular appearances at conferences, strong scholarship, robust experience as a campus leader, and long years as a Writing Across the Curriculum (WAC) advocate at many levels, Steve prefers to operate below the radar. Therefore, this interview will expose him as the WAC expert he truly is.

Through professional conferences, I gradually became aware of Steve's remarkable range as a teacher and scholar. I am honored to have appeared on a number of conference panels with him, often at the annual convention of the Council of Writing Program Administrators. We share an approach to faculty development that we both find rewarding in itself as well as a vehicle for spreading the teaching practices that undergird WAC. One visible outcome of our commitment to faculty development and WAC was an invitation to write a chapter defining faculty development for the 2013 volume, *A Rhetoric for Writing Program Administrators*, edited by Rita Malenczyk. Doing so was a pleasure.

Steve did his undergraduate work at the University of Kentucky, earned an MA in English and creative writing from the University of Louisville, and completed a doctorate in composition studies at Indiana University. His post-doctorate career has been spent at the University of Dayton in Ohio, and, as readers will soon see, his work has varied a great deal. Steve's career shows how WAC thinking, teaching, and evangelizing inform professional success. As Steve's work demonstrates, WAC in its broadest applications transforms institutions. Steve would not make that claim, thanks to his persistent modesty. Read on for the evidence and make your own judgment.

This interview was compiled through e-mail correspondence and mutual editing over several weeks in early 2014.

Carol Rutz: When you completed your graduate work in the late 1980s, did you expect WAC to require much of your attention? What led you to WAC?

Steve Wilhoit: A couple of things have led me in this direction—it's been more of an evolution than anything else. When I finished graduate work at Indiana University in 1988, I was hired by folks at the University of Dayton to be the English department's first comp/rhet specialist and to run the Teaching Assistant (TA) education program, which I did for twelve years along with completing a couple of stints as Writing Program Administrator (WPA). Over those years, I did a few faculty development workshops on writing-to-learn theories and strategies, which were pretty well attended by faculty from across the curriculum. They were largely just extensions of what I was doing with the TAs.

CR: Ah, so you were plunged into WAC waters early on—and you must have been very busy.

SW: Yeah, those first few years were pretty busy, partly because I was also running a longitudinal study of writing at The University of Dayton (UD). Since I was new to the school, I had no idea what kinds of writing assignments or projects our students completed as they moved through their majors or whether our composition program prepared them at all for that work. I ended up having fifteen students participate in the study, each majoring in a different subject. These students agreed to give me a copy of every writing assignment they completed in every class they took at UD—preferably with the instructors' grade and comments on them—to complete a questionnaire about their writing experiences at the end of every term, and to sit for an interview at the end of each academic year. All of them completed the project with me—bless their hearts.

CR: Good for them! What did you learn?

SW: I got a glimpse into how student writing assignments changed by major and year in school at UD and a better idea of how faculty were and were not using writing to promote student learning. I began to incorporate those insights into the faculty workshops I offered. Then around 2000, I decided to organize a semester-long WAC seminar for faculty and staff. About a dozen colleagues signed up. I thought the previous occasional workshops had been helpful, but I wanted to offer an extended examination of WAC for a small group of interested faculty. I figured that over the term, the participants could actually test the theories or apply the strategies we discussed and report the results back to the group. The best way to overcome faculty doubts or hesitancy about WAC is for them to discover its benefits for themselves in the classes they teach. Plus, trying new things is scary for many faculty members, so having a peer support group was important.

CR: And what happened?

SW: The seminar was more successful than I anticipated—those initial participants were really happy with the results and talked up the program. I approached our school's associate provost for learning initiatives to see about support for a second seminar, and she loved the idea. She invited me to hold the seminar in our new Learning Teaching Center and even found some money to pay the participants a small stipend. We were off and running, and I still offer the seminar every year.

After that, I became increasingly involved in the work of the Learning Teaching Center, offering workshops and seminars on a range of topics—assessment, creative writing, critical thinking, graduate student education, and technology. All of these were really "spin offs" of that first writing across the curriculum seminar. Over time, I found myself transitioning from writing program administration to faculty development—via WAC. Eventually, I was asked to become an associate director of the Learning Teaching Center and head the Office of Writing, Research, and New Media. Now I split my time every term between the Center and the English Department, kind of jumping from office to office.

CR: Staying busy, I see. Turning to your publications, they include a popular guide for TA training as teachers of rhetoric and composition. What experiences led you to write that book, and how does it engage WAC? When you train graduate student teaching assistants, do you explicitly introduce them to WAC?

SW: Right—the TA book grew out of all the years I worked with the teaching assistants in our department. The question is interesting because I wouldn't say that I explicitly introduced the TAs to WAC—that "WAC" was a topic on a syllabus or something, but I can't imagine preparing someone to teach introductory college writing courses outside of the context of WAC. Composition programs can accomplish a lot of things—or try to accomplish them, at least—and can be used as a means to a lot of ends—but I think primary among them is helping students make the transition from high school to college writing and preparing them as best we can for the kinds of writing tasks they are likely to be assigned in their other college classes.

CR: Not everyone thinks about it that way. Some would say that first-year composition (FYC) should be about writing, per se, not necessarily writing in the larger college or academic context.

SW: Right—WAC is about understanding that context. Writing *across* the curriculum—whose curriculum, what curriculum? FYC doesn't stand outside of an institution's or a major's or a student's curriculum—it's a key part of one or all of them. Even if a first-year writing course does not specifically address that larger academic context, it's taking place *within* it. I think writing teachers benefit from understanding that context, and that certainly influenced my work with the TAs.

CR: Let's talk about another teaching site. You are one of the few WAC people that I know of who has worked with local high schools on WAC at the secondary level. Tell that story—how did you get involved?

SW: It was really just a matter of local circumstances and saying yes to opportunities. I live in Oakwood, a small community just south of Dayton. Oakwood is a pretty close-knit community. It's got two elementary schools, one high school, no school buses—most kids walk to school and walk home for lunch. My three daughters all attended school in Oakwood, and over those years I got to know a lot of the teachers, the high school principal, and the school superintendent pretty well. In fact, a few of my daughters' teachers are former students of mine. Anyway, at some point, the principal and school superintendent asked if I would run a workshop for their teachers on how writing can promote student learning (I'd run similar workshops for the Dayton Public Schools). That workshop was well received; so they asked me back a few times. Eventually, the high school faculty and administrators decided they wanted to put together a coherent WAC program that would help guide writing instruction across the curriculum for grades 9-12 and asked me to lend a hand. That turned into the OWL Program—Oakwood Writing to Learn. Conversations then turned to how the school could best support student writing and they created a writing center in the high school's library. Finally, assessment became an issue, and I worked with the teachers and principal to create a rubric that faculty could use to evaluate writing across the curriculum, grades 9-12. These projects just followed one another pretty naturally.

CR: Has any research come out of that effort?

SW: I co-authored an article on OWL with the superintendent and an English teacher.

CR: How did high school teachers respond?

SW: The teachers in Oakwood are terrific—really smart and dedicated. Teachers from across the curriculum—English, math, physics, music, history, biology, you name it—built the curriculum and support systems. A lot of my work was just framing conversations, asking questions, offering feedback, and helping the faculty identify ways to build on what they were already doing in their classes.

CR: What evidence do the schools have that WAC serves their students?

SW: The assessments carried out in the high school show that these programs have been tremendously effective. Yearly, Oakwood is ranked as the best or second best high school in the state, particularly in math, science, and writing. Not surprisingly, the math and science teachers played—and continue to play—a central role in OWL. Another form of assessment: One day my oldest daughter complained about all the writing she had to do in her science classes—"Is that *your* fault?" she asked me.

CR: You have mentioned your close association with the University of Dayton's Ryan C. Harris Learning Teaching Center. How did that appointment come about?

SW: The Ryan C. Harris Learning Teaching Center (LTC) opened at the University of Dayton about a dozen years ago. It's located on the ground floor of the library and is unique because it consolidates a wide range of support services for both students and faculty in one location. Student learning support, instructional technologies, and faculty development—it's all located there. As I said earlier, I first became involved with the LTC when we moved the WAC seminar there. As the number and types of workshops and presentations I did in the LTC increased, I was named an LTC Fellow which allowed the associate provost who runs the place to buy out some of my classes and garner me some release time. To help facilitate my work, I eventually got an office in the LTC and then, when the place reorganized about 5-6 years ago, I was asked to officially become one of three assistant directors.

CR: Including your faculty development work, is it fair to say that WAC has influenced your career trajectory?

SW: Coming out of grad school and joining the English Department, I had no idea I'd eventually be doing this work. But, looking back, there's a logic to how things have progressed. My last couple of years in graduate school, I was a peer mentor to new TAs. Then I became Director of TA Training and WPA when I moved to the English Department at Dayton. That work led to offering WAC workshops for university and high school faculty and then to doing a wide range of faculty development work in the LTC. In my mind, it's all just various forms of teaching. Teaching undergraduate students, grad students, and faculty—all of it is mutually supporting. My training and education in rhetoric, along with my experience as a WPA and involvement with WAC, was the best preparation I could receive for work in faculty development. Looking around, professionally a whole lot of us are making this move—an awful lot of the leaders in faculty development have backgrounds in rhetoric, composition, and WAC. The skills transfer really well.

CR: Speaking of teaching and transferring skills, you and I recently gave a one-day workshop on faculty development at the annual conference of the Council of

Writing Program Administrators. We emphasized that a good faculty workshop requires effective teaching on the part of the leaders. As you review your experience as a teacher of faculty colleagues, can you articulate a philosophy of faculty development?

SW: Yeah—that was a very fun and productive workshop, wasn't it? This idea came up a couple of times in discussions that day—when doing faculty development work, you have to balance two important forms of service. On the one hand, you try to help faculty improve at the work they do—help them do it more effectively, more efficiently, in a more self-aware manner, etc. But on the other hand, you want to advocate for needed changes—you sometimes try to persuade faculty to do things differently than they do them now or to do different things all together. Support and advocacy—improving what is and pushing for what should be—both are crucial aspects of faculty development. To do this kind of work well, I think you need to combine effective teaching techniques with the principles of servant leadership. Faculty development is just another form of teaching and one key to effective teaching is to understand it as a rhetorical act. What are the best instructional practices to employ given the people I'm working with, what we all hope to get out of the experience, the reason we're all together, etc.? Along with that, servant leadership is also involved. For me—and I know this is a great simplification of a complex set of theories and practices—but for me, a servant leader's first impulse is to ask "How can I help?" To answer this question, you have to be quiet and listen—listen carefully, empathetically, and discerningly. What is it, exactly, I can do to move things forward or assist the process? That can include helping someone figure out precisely what it is they want or need. Once we figure that out, we can move forward together.

Now, the flip side of that is filling the role of advocate or instigator or change agent. If you assume that role in faculty development, you better be sure to know what you're about, what you hope to accomplish, and why. You need to articulate a guiding vision for the change you hope to bring about that will entice others to join in. Then, again, you rely on the principles of servant leadership and your skills as a rhetorician to bring about that end.

CR: As a person steeped in both teaching and administration, you are known for showing colleagues how people in that dual situation have opportunities to explore and exhibit leadership. Explain what you mean—the kind(s) of leadership and the ways faculty/administrators, including WAC directors, can become effective leaders. What challenges need to be overcome?

SW: Too often, those of us involved in composition, WAC, or TA education programs see ourselves as managers rather than leaders. I mean, what do we often call ourselves? Writing program *administrators*. Good administration of any academic program is important and difficult work. Not everyone has the skills needed to do it well. But when we conceive of administration solely or largely as management, we shortchange ourselves. Leadership is different than management. Leaders inspire others to join them in pursuit of a shared vision. And any of us can be more effective leaders, whether we hold a position of authority or not.

For the past decade, I've been part of a leadership training program for faculty, staff, and administrators at the University of Dayton. I think the biggest step people have to take to become more effective leaders is to better understand what leadership really entails. It's not about power or authority or position; it's about facilitating change through service, collaboration, and caring; it's about building consensus and community around a shared vision or goal. Sometimes you take charge and lead from the front; most of the time you don't—you lead by enabling others, by facilitating change, by setting the example. Leadership is a form of service. Effective leaders listen more than they talk. They clarify the situation at hand, anticipate and articulate the challenges, and work with others to find a way forward.

CR: What other circumstances favor the development of leadership potential?

SW: Effective leaders also have a good sense of timing—they know when to speak up in a meeting, when to make a proposal, when to back off, and when to push forward. That's a hard lesson to learn—to hold off until it's the right time to act. Sometimes that's knowing when to speak up during a committee meeting—when you can move the group past a hurdle or around a stumbling block. Other times it's knowing when to make a proposal to the department, chair, or dean, and how to present that proposal effectively when you do. It's understanding your audience and the context.

CR: You are a swimmer and a coach. Is that more WAC in action? How does swimming fit with your life and work?

SW: Yeah—after twelve years, I'm about to "retire" as a volunteer high school swim coach. This season is my last hurrah. I'll still coach kids in the summer at our community pool (I get to work with the little kids—4-6 years old—they're a hoot).

I love to swim, always have. Growing up, I spent almost every free minute I had at Lakeside Swim Club in Louisville. And all of my daughters grew up swimming and swam through high school. Two swam in college. But as with so many other things in my life, I stumbled into coaching without planning to. My daughters all swam in a summer league at our community pool. I was there one morning with them and saw that a high school student I knew was having a hard time trying to coach two lanes of very young children. I asked her if she wanted me to help. Seventeen years later, I'm still coaching.

CR: So you see coaching as teaching?

SW: Coaching, teaching—they're the same thing. The processes are essentially the same. You're helping people learn a set of skills. Let's stick with swimming. If I'm going to help someone improve their stroke, I'm going to have them swim a little bit while I watch. Allowing lots of room for individual style, there are certain basic mechanics of an effective stroke. You can watch someone swim and analyze their stroke in terms of those mechanics—their head or body position, their kick, their catch, their pull, their recovery, their turn, etc. You can then figure out a game plan for that swimmer, the changes the swimmer needs to make to improve and the order you tackle them in. If you try to change everything at once, the whole thing falls apart. It's too much to focus on—better to just focus on one thing at a time. When you see progress, you move on to the next thing on your list. You offer instruction, give feedback, and have them practice, practice, practice. Over time—faster for some, slower for others—if they stick with it, they become better swimmers.

But as a coach you also have to provide emotional support and motivation; you have to acknowledge and praise any and every improvement, no matter how small. If I'm working with a child who won't put her face in the water, for example, I make sure to celebrate the first time she manages it, even if it's just for a second. Then we'll work on getting her to do it for an entire stroke, then for a couple of strokes, and so on. In the end, you can't beat the feeling of watching a kid you coach put it all together in the pool. And they know it, too. It suddenly feels right and they are gliding beautifully through the water, performing without thinking about it, letting muscle memory take over.

CR: OK, pull that example into WAC for me.

SW: Sure. Helping an eight-year-old third-grader learn how to do a back-stroke flip turn, or an eighteen-year-old college student learn how to put together an effective sentence, or a forty-eight-year-old colleague learn how to promote student learning through writing—fundamentally it's all pretty much the same. Figure out where they are, work out an idea of where you and they want to be, and help them get there in whatever time you have to work with them. And if you manage to do it right, if you help them understand what you're doing and why, years after you're gone, they'll continue to teach themselves.

CR: Let's hope that WAC consistently works that way—for students and faculty. Thank you, Steve.

SW: Thank you. It's been great talking with you.

Works Cited

Koening, Anne, Mary Jo Scalzo, and Stephen Wilhoit. "Writing Across the Curriculum—Starting from Scratch." *Today's Schools* 3.4 (2003): 15-18. Print.

Malencyzk, Rita, ed. *A Rhetoric for Writing Program Administrators*. Anderson, SC: Parlor Press, 2013. Print.

Wihoit, Stephen W. *The Longman Teaching Assistant's Handbook: A Guide for Graduate Instructors of Writing and Literature*. New York: Pearson, 2008. Print.

The Tables Are Turned:
Carol Rutz

TERRY MYERS ZAWACKI

The tables are turned, Carol Rutz. When I suggested to Roy Andrews and Carol that she herself was long overdue as the subject of a Writing Across the Curriculum (WAC)-leader profile, she recalled that I'd made this table-turning "threat"—or promise, as I prefer to call it—back in 2007 when she interviewed me for what has become, since her 2003 interview with John Bean, a regular feature in *The WAC Journal*. Well, it's taken me seven years to fulfill that promise, but with this interview, I'm happy to say, readers will now have the opportunity to learn more about Carol's impressive background as a scholar, teacher, and director of Carleton College's highly regarded The Writing Program, which has been recognized every year since 2006 in the *US News and World Report* college issue as one of the best in the country for writing in the disciplines.

While Carleton's WAC genealogy dates back to 1974 when the college is credited with being the first to establish cross-curricular writing requirements and to hold workshops to prepare faculty across the disciplines to teach with writing, the program was languishing when Carol became director in 1997. She set out to change that state of affairs, starting by working with key colleagues to secure grant funding to develop a sophomore portfolio requirement that involved extensive faculty development and a now nationally recognized writing assessment process (Condon and Rutz 373-74). The portfolio initiative proved to be so successful that it provided data for a quantitative reasoning initiative, which Carol and colleagues quickly and astutely linked to the importance of using data rhetorically to make effective arguments and which has now become another hallmark of her many WAC accomplishments at Carleton.

As those of us in WAC know well, collaboration is at the heart of our program-building work; that Carol is a consummate collaborator can be seen not only in her programmatic accomplishments at Carleton but also in her scholarship. Of the forty-plus "selected publications" she lists on her CV, nearly all are co-authored, including, for example, the 2007 co-edited collection *Building Intellectual Community through Collaboration*. While Carol may be best known for her scholarship on writing assessment, WAC, and quantitative reasoning, she's also written widely on faculty and WAC program development, most recently with Bill Condon in the 2012 *College Composition and Communication* article "A Taxonomy of Writing Across the Curriculum Programs: Evolving to Serve Broader Agendas." And, of course, she has contributed her deftly conducted interviews with WAC professionals to *The WAC Journal* for the past twelve issues, counting this one.

Having noted Carol's skill as an interviewer over the years, I confess that I felt some trepidation about whether I could meet the high bar she has set, so my first step was to call her to ask how the interview series got started and how the heck she does it so well. It wasn't intended to be a series, she said, just an interview with John Bean, which she thought would be fun to do since he's "so famous and yet so modest," but Roy Andrews, *The WAC Journal* editor, liked the interview and asked for more of the same. Speaking of modesty, Carol told me that the questions she asks come out of "twenty years of hanging out and having the honor of associating with lots of really good colleagues." So, she advised me, I should just start with the highlights of the person's career and then turn it over to the interviewee to let responses to one question lead to another and another, and then all I had to do was "go back and insert transitional questions to amplify and clarify." How easy, she makes it sound, but how expertly she does it.

Terry Zawacki: How did you get started in WAC?

Carol Rutz: I was fortunate to do my graduate work at the University of Minnesota (U of MN) at a time when composition program teaching assistants from all over the university were trained to teach required writing courses at two levels: first-year writing and junior-level courses tailored to disciplinary areas; Writing for the Arts, Writing for the Social Sciences, Critical Reading and Writing for Management, and Writing about Science. The advanced courses made a lot of sense to me, even though I would have preferred to see disciplinary faculty teaching them—which is now the case in Minnesota's new Writing Enriched-Curriculum. I benefited from teaching courses at more than one level with more than one disciplinary emphasis, and through doing so I became a WAC groupie.

TZ: So your interest in teaching science-related writing courses dates back to your training as a TA. Any other influences?

CR: As I said, I had the chance at Minnesota to teach upper division writing courses, and two of my favorites were Writing about Science and Writing for the Health Professions. I gravitated toward them thanks to my family of origin. Both of my parents were teachers; my mother taught first grade and my father taught biology at a small liberal arts college for nearly forty years. He was a field biologist with expertise in entomology, evolution, and animal behavior. Consequently, my brother and I were immersed in field study by default. For example, walking to church included commentary on and the capture of interesting insects that were poisoned in a little pocket bottle, dumped out on Dad's desk in the evening, labeled, and pinned as specimens in cigar boxes lined with balsa wood. We couldn't observe that ritual, among others, and not pick up a lot of knowledge through question and answer as well as flat-out osmosis.

In college, I majored in English but took several biology courses, served as a lab assistant, and often worked summers doing menial fieldwork for research projects. The most memorable of those was the summer I worked for a parasitologist on two projects: one on the parasites of wild ducks and the other on the leeches of Minnesota. For the first, I dissected freshly-killed ducks, isolating, identifying, and preserving all parasites, including liver flukes, tapeworms, and other dainties. For the second, I stomped around various lakes in chest waders, overturning rocks and logs to collect and preserve leeches. As you might imagine, this job required overcoming an atavistic aversion to these bloodsuckers. I take pride in getting past the "ick" factor. Anyone who wants the lowdown on the four species of Minnesota freshwater leeches should give me a call.

Much later, I worked for eight years for a residential treatment center for psychotic adolescents as the medical records person. I learned a lot there about psychotherapy and developmental theory, and I also earned certification as a medical records professional. As a result of these varied experiences, I have a brain tuned to the scientific method, and when WAC called, I was happiest at first to answer in a scientific idiom. At Carleton, in addition to WAC outreach to scientists, I have been fortunate to team teach with an astrophysicist as well as develop a course for environmental studies on public rhetoric and environmental science.

TZ: You've written extensively about faculty development, and clearly, you enjoy teaming with faculty in other disciplines to develop and teach courses. What experiences equipped you with the confidence to work with your peers across the curriculum on how to teach effectively with writing?

CR: Your question takes me back to graduate school once again. I was an elderly grad student with considerable experience in the work world when I showed up at the U of MN in 1992—I was the second oldest person in my cohort. I paid close attention to TA training and learned a great deal from it. After a few quarters of teaching and observing fellow TAs as they taught, I decided to apply for an administrative job on the team that planned and delivered TA training. I was also invited to work with Chris Anson, who directed Minnesota's composition program at the time, on a dual enrolment program called College in the Schools. He and I planned and delivered workshops for the high school teachers who taught the equivalent of the Minnesota first-year writing course in their schools for college credit.

Those years of TA training and working with (and observing) the high school teachers persuaded me that faculty are the smartest, best, and most challenging students anyone could ask for. As such, they deserve the best that leaders have to offer—a message that Steve Wilhoit from the University of Dayton and I tried to convey last summer for the Writing Programs Administrator (WPA) workshop on faculty development. Teaching one's peers cannot be done on the fly. Careful preparation of materials and respect for that audience foster a positive climate for learning on the part of all involved. All of this boils down to a personal mission to take all students seriously, from the nervous fall term frosh to the seasoned and brilliant colleague.

TZ: Even with this background, it must have been a little daunting to take on the direction of the very first WAC program in the country. According to Chuck Bazerman and his co-authors' *Reference Guide to Writing Across the Curriculum*, for example, not only was Carleton's the first WAC program but also, in 1975, Carleton's program was the subject of one of the first accounts of WAC as a writing movement in an article written by Harriet Sheridan in the *ADE Bulletin*: "Teaching Writing Extra-territorially: Carleton College." And, in yet another first, Carleton's program linked peer tutors with Writing in the Disciplines (WID) courses, a model Sheridan brought to Brown University when she established their Writing Fellows program (Bazerman et al 26, 110). Can you tell us about your own first steps when you took over direction of what you and Bill Condon characterized as a static program in your "Taxonomy" article?

CR: Terry, what you don't know is that I have a complicated relationship with Carleton. I worked there as a staff member in several different jobs for about ten years before I decided to do grad school. I left assuming I would not be back. I hoped to finish the degree and find a job somewhere, doing something that involved teaching writing. To my great surprise, just as I was finishing my dissertation research, a part-time, one-year position opened up at Carleton, and friends encouraged me to apply. I'd been gone five years, and I contacted the associate dean in charge of the search to see if my application would be welcomed. I was urged to interview and I got the job, which was mostly faculty development in WAC, complete with an office, a computer, and time to work on my dissertation. That one-year stint developed into a hybrid administrative-teaching position, and I'm still there.

In addition to the good fortune of landing a job, I returned to a place with which I was already well acquainted and also knew where the bodies were buried. Furthermore, I was supervised by associate dean Elizabeth Ciner, a lively and imaginative career administrator with a background in writing instruction as part of her own graduate study. Neither of us knew much about assessment, but we did know that Carleton had outgrown part of the innovative early WAC model described in the Sheridan piece you cite. Assessment was that program's weakness, as Clara Hardy, Bill Condon, and I explain in a 2002 piece in *The WAC Journal* ("WAC for the Long Haul: A Tale of Hope"). It was Liz Ciner who latched on to an invitation from the Bush Foundation in St. Paul to submit a proposal for faculty development that would address our WAC program somehow. She wrote the planning grant, and I wrote most of the subsequent full grant proposal, which was funded for three years and renewed for three more. The goal of the planning grant was to learn about writing assessment; to do so we invited Bill Condon, Marty Townsend, and Kathleen Blake Yancey to campus to work with faculty, writing tutors, and our Learning and Teaching Center to educate us. Prepared by those brilliant tutorials, we were able to put together a proposal that linked faculty development to writing assessment through the vehicle of a sophomore portfolio.

For the full proposal, we were wise enough to request course releases for three senior faculty to do a lot of the heavy lifting as we extended education about writing assessment through faculty workshops, brown bags, visiting speakers, and the faculty governance system. Neither Liz nor I were tenure-able, and we were well aware of the need to proceed carefully. Our faculty ambassadors from classics, economics, and physics and astronomy represented the program, answered questions, offered reasoned positions, and defused anxiety. They also took a fair amount of flak, and for that I owe them my profound gratitude. Without their collaboration and persistence, writing assessment at Carleton would look very different than it does today.

TZ: While the influence of Kathi Yancey and Bill Condon can be seen in your decision to use portfolio assessment, what made you decide that a sophomore portfolio was the place to begin? Why not a junior or senior portfolio, in other words?

CR: Carleton's previous writing assessment was often postponed until the eve of graduation, effectively pulling whatever teeth the writing requirement had. The decision on writing proficiency came through one course (any WAC course) and was rendered by one professor, period. Most students passed easily, yet they complained that the requirement was inconsistent and arbitrary. Faculty complained that students did not take it seriously. Everyone was right.

Therefore, we wanted to place the assessment early enough in a student's career that shortcomings could be addressed as the student worked through advanced courses in the major as well as the capstone. Carleton students declare a major at the end of the sophomore year. Timing the portfolio assessment to coincide makes sense to students and gives faculty a heads up if new majors have writing weaknesses as evidenced through the portfolio.

TZ: Carleton's assessment process has been recognized by the National Council of Teachers of English (NCTE) and the Council of Writing Program Administrators in a white paper and in their gallery of model programs (http://wpacouncil.org/CarletonColl). While readers may be familiar with your portfolio assessment process (or can read about it on the WPA site), I'm interested in what has drawn you to writing assessment as a process and as the subject of much of your scholarship. What's most interesting and engaging to you about assessing writing?

CR: Maybe it's engaging because I learned about it out of exigency. It was the work that had to be addressed when I came on board in my current role, and there was no avoiding it. Now that I sort of get it, I tend to be a bit evangelistic. Connecting assessment with faculty development would never have occurred to me had we not worked closely with the Bush Foundation. Having to plan activities within the grant budget and report annually on results focused the work. As I wrote those reports and contracted with visitors and planned workshops, I could perceive the college changing around me. Assessment became—in most of my colleagues' minds—a means of enacting their strong sense of responsibility to their students. For them to encounter student work in the variety that a college-wide portfolio makes possible meant that they actively sought out colleagues with innovative assignments. Talking about teaching and specifically about teaching writing has taken on an importance that I did not imagine to be possible. Consequently, courses and assignments exhibit more specific, measurable goals, and faculty have adopted teaching practices to improve their students' experience.

Simply put, I speak and write about assessment with the convert's zeal—particularly as it informs faculty development.

TZ: In your and Bill Condon's "Taxonomy" article, you note that the sophomore portfolio became a model for quantitative reasoning across the curriculum. Will you talk a bit about the Quantitative Inquiry, Reasoning, and Knowledge (QuIRK) initiative you've been involved in? What is it and what is your role?

CR: Conversations about what we now call QuIRK originated in the early 2000s among natural scientists who lamented the disinclination of students to apply their knowledge of mathematics in courses that followed, say, the calculus sequence. Faculty were frustrated by having to re-teach concepts and techniques. As discussion continued, the focus shifted from sophisticated math knowledge to the use of data as evidence in arguments as a measure of critical thinking. The typical example: no one can read *The New York Times* without knowing how to read a graph, as well as interpret ratios, percentages, and claims about probability. This version of quantitative literacy spoke eloquently to social scientists, particularly in psychology and economics, who picked up the ball and ran with it.

Research on quantitative literacy (QL) or quantitative reasoning (QR) programs elsewhere revealed that most schools administered a test to new students during orientation and directed those who performed poorly to a QR or QL course to cover the basics. As I attended these discussions, I was thrilled to hear my colleagues observe that "inoculation" was inappropriate for true QL, citing literature that urged across-the-curriculum programs in QL—similar to WAC. But, the question became, how to fund a program with WAC-ish machinery that would have to educate faculty broadly and provide some sort of assessment.

At this point, a colleague in geology piped up and observed that the sophomore portfolio welcomes data-driven prose. We could grab a random sample of student papers and look at them. We did, and we learned that students did a fine job of using QR when the assignment specifically required it. If they were not cued, they not only overlooked QR, but they passed up opportunities to use it, even if their sources were QR-laden. This evidence, based in writing assessment, proved persuasive for funding.

My role has ranged from sponsoring early WAC/QR workshops (before QuIRK had funding) to learning how to import QR into my writing courses to participating in QR assessment to continuing to co-sponsor workshops. I have consistently served on the ad hoc collective that administers QuIRK. What I have learned has transformed my teaching by pointing students toward the power of data to lend precision and authority to their work.

TZ: I know you've been working with John Bean in the area of writing and quantitative reasoning. How did you two happen to begin working together on QuIRK initiatives?

CR: I don't remember exactly how our collaboration all went down, but I was able to interest John in putting together a workshop on Writing With Numbers. The emphasis, you will not be surprised to learn, was on using data rhetorically. For example, he would provide a table from the U.S. Census, and we worked in groups to find the "stories" in that table and express them as arguments. We've had variations on that workshop at Carleton several times, including a recent one on Speaking With Numbers. Before his recent retirement and after working with Carleton faculty, John Bean was doing a lot of work on QR at Seattle University, where he was their long-time WAC director. He has published on some of that work with colleagues from both natural science and finance programs.

I'm planning a workshop soon on responding to student writing (everyone's favorite anxiety) with attention to helping students improve their use of data as evidence. As I slowly learn more about statistics, I am getting better about responding to students' attempts to employ data rhetorically. Many of my colleagues are way ahead of me, and I think the workshop could benefit all of us.

TZ: You clearly have plenty on your plate, but I'm wondering if you have another project in the works that you'd like to talk about.

CR: Well, yes. Carleton has landed external grants for a bunch of curricular initiatives. In addition to WAC and QuIRK, we have or have had programs in Visual Learning, Global Engagement, Arts and Technology, Civic Engagement, and more. These efforts have offered students and faculty rich educational experiences. However, the only ones that are staffed and have budget lines are WAC and Civic Engagement. When funding lapses, either the initiative limps along informally for a while, or perhaps a faculty member accepts short-term leadership responsibility, compensated by a course release and a summer stipend. Because our colleagues are energetic and scrupulous, this system sort of works. However, groups can find themselves at odds over support staff, workshop dates, facilities, scheduling speakers, and other programming efforts that splinter audiences and dilute the effectiveness of the programs. As independent contractors, faculty enjoy being in charge of their programs. To some extent, alas, the autonomy that faculty cherish is preserved at the cost of the big picture.

I am trying to make the case that we could achieve some administrative and programmatic coherence through something like a Communication Across Campus (CXC) Program that would coordinate as many initiatives as are willing plus formalize an initiative on public speaking and fold in some co-curricular programs. Communication can mean pretty much anything, right? Both our institutional assessment plan and our strategic plan emphasize communication, broadly construed, so a foundation exists. Whether this idea will sell in any general way remains to be seen.

TZ: Well, building a new program is certainly an ambitious undertaking, especially when added to all that you're currently doing, including, if I may shift focus, your contributions to *The WAC Journal*, as a member of the editorial board and as author of the regularly featured WAC-leader interviews. You've now conducted twelve interviews. How do you decide whom to interview? And whom would you still like to interview?

CR: It varies. I ask people I know well, trying to vary gender, kind of school, scholarly interests, age, and so on. As is my habit, I work through relationships. So far, no one has turned me down. Call it a lack of imagination, but I would hesitate to interview someone I do not know. Why? Because I would have a hard time knowing what to ask without some shared personal connections. I'm glad you asked whom I'd still like to interview because I am kicking myself that I never interviewed Greg Colomb, who, as you know, died way too young. We became close friends, personally and professionally, and his work has influenced me a great deal. I miss him.

TZ: Is there any one thing you've learned from all those good WAC colleagues that really stands out for you?

CR: All of the interviewees have been generous with their time and shown abundant interest in everything. They have also cracked me up in one way or another. Laughing with friends is always a good thing. I've learned in detail about programs at other places, mostly large universities, which helps me put our work at a tiny place like Carleton in perspective. I'm in awe of what some of our colleagues, yourself included, have accomplished at huge universities with required writing courses, hordes of graduate students, and, increasingly, large numbers of adjuncts. I have none of that to manage at Carleton. Partly as a result of the interviews, I see my campus as a small laboratory where an experiment in connecting assessment and faculty development has succeeded. The same experiment might well have failed in a larger institutional context with fewer campus-wide relationships.

Works Cited

Bazerman, C., Little, J., Bethel, L., Chavkin, Little, Joseph, Bethel, Lisa, Chavkin, T., Fouquette, D. & Garufis, J. (2005). *Reference Guide to Writing Across the Curriculum*. Fort Collins, CO: Parlor Press and The WAC Clearinghouse. Available at http://wac.colostate.edu/books/bazerman_wac/.

Condon, W. & Rutz, C. (2012). A Taxonomy of writing across the curriculum programs: Evolving to serve broader agendas. *College Composition and Communication* 64(2), 357-382.

Council of Writing Program Administrators (2010). *WPA Assessment Gallery: Assessment Models*. Available at http://wpacouncil.org/CarletonColl.

Rutz, C., Hardy, C., & Condon, W. (2002). WAC for the long haul: A tale of hope. *The WAC Journal* 13, 7-16.

Sheridan, H. (1974). *Teaching writing extra-territorially: Carleton College*. ADE Bulletin 44, 32.

Review

MYA POE

Kathleen Blake Yancey, Liane Robertson, and Kara Taczak. *Writing Across Contexts: Transfer, Composition, and Sites of Writing.* Utah State UP, 2014. 191 pages.

The topic of transfer is undeniably one of the hottest topics in composition studies today. Transfer, though, is a knotty subject—one that begs us to consider such questions as: What do we mean when we study transfer in writing, how do we study transfer, and ultimately, is it possible to teach transfer? To answer these questions, I think it's useful to consider what researchers, such as Kathleen Blake Yancey, Liane Robertson, and Kara Taczak in *Writing Across Contexts: Transfer, Composition, and Sites of Writing,* are attempting to do in the context of the composition research tradition on writing development and assessment.

Transfer research isn't simply about writing development as Yancey et al. demonstrate. For them, it's also about what we should be teaching. I see this union as bringing together sociocultural research on writing development, circa 1990s–present, with more recent assessment pressures placed on writing program administrators, circa 2000s to the present. Methodologically what this means is that, in contrast to longitudinal research on writing development that looks across college writing experiences (e.g., Beaufort, 2007; Herrington & Curtis, 2000; Sommers & Saltz, 2004; Sternglass, 1997; Walvoord & McCarthy, 1990), research on transfer (e.g., Bergmann & Zepernick, 2007; Jarratt et al., 2009; Nowacek, 2011; Reiff & Bawarshi, 2011; Wardle, 2007), and emerging threshold research (Adler-Kassner et al., 2012), question what we should be teaching in first-year writing to promote the transfer of writing knowledge.

Now, the need to justify first-year writing is not a new question, as David Russell and others have pointed out. What's different today is that composition studies—as a bonafide academic discipline—can claim a certain expertise about writing. We know a lot about writing development and writing assessment. And that's important given the external assessment pressures placed on us, especially in relation to retention and graduation. A craft or practitioner sensibility (e.g., Murray's *The Craft of Revision,* 1990; Elbow's *Writing Without Teachers*) just doesn't cut it today for many writing program administrators. We need to claim our expertise on the subject of writing to retain control of our curricula.

In bringing us the first book-length study of transfer in composition studies, Yancey, Robertson, and Taczak provide us a contemporary view of such exigences surrounding writing research today. Their project was guided by two questions:

"What difference does the content in composition make in the transfer of writing knowledge and practices and how can reflection as a systematic activity keyed to transfer support students' continued writing development?" (p. 33). As they explain, their project was "a detailed research study into the efficacy of a certain kind of curriculum intending to facilitate students' transfer of writing knowledge and practice" (p. 33). It was also a "synthetic account of scholarship" as well as a "text theorizing transfer of writing knowledge and practice" (p. 34). The impetus to study the efficacy of a particular curriculum, thus, is really an assessment question delivered in a grounded qualitative method.

The curriculum studied was a model developed at Florida State University by Yancey and colleagues called Teaching for Transfer (TFT), which is based on four features: "key terms, theoretical readings, writing in multiple genres, and reflective practice" (p. 35). Yancey, Robertson, and Taczak offer a clear rationale for each of the four features in the TFT curriculum (of which I found the rationale for "key terms" most interesting but also most problematic because I'm not convinced that academic terms are the best key terms for everyday writers). The researchers studied seven participants in three classes: three students in a TFT course, two students in an expressivist-styled course, and two students in a media and culture-themed first-year writing course. Students were interviewed over two semesters—the semester they were in the writing course, which was the second of two required first-year writing courses, and the following semester when they enrolled in general education courses. Teachers of the three first-year writing courses were also interviewed and an analysis of course materials and student writing was conducted.

The findings of the TFT study point to four conclusions. First, students who have been successful writers have little incentive to change their relationship to writing or writing practices, regardless of the course curriculum. In short, students transfer their writing identities from previous schooling experiences. Second, some students are able to reflect and reassemble their writing practices due to failed transfer or critical incidents. Third, courses that do not make writing content explicit leave students with the perception that first-year writing is disconnected from other university writing. Finally, a first-year writing course that asks students to develop their own theory of writing and to reflect on that theory through multiple avenues can be a vehicle—for some students—to transfer writing knowledge to other contexts. This was especially clear in situations where students were writing concurrently in various classes.

Following the chapter on the TFT study is a chapter on how students make use of prior knowledge. This chapter introduces us to students not profiled in the previous chapter but who were part of the TFT class. What I liked best about *Writing Across Contexts: Transfer, Composition, and Sites of Writing* was this discussion of how students use prior knowledge in shaping their subsequent uptake, or not, of writing instruction. Here, the theorizing is rich and the case studies illuminating. For example, Yancey et al. write about the role of assessment as a "point of departure" in students' conceptions of themselves as writers and its influence on learning to write: "Without their own standards for assessing their work, students participating in this study were also especially sensitive to grades" (p. 107). Drawing on Applebee and Langer's research (2011), they go on to explain how narrow conceptions of writing found in high school often leave students "absent prior knowledge" about many genres of writing commonly found in college, although they make no speculations as to how the Common Core State Standards might change this landscape.

In conclusion, Yancey et al. offer six recommendations for effective teaching for transfer in first-year writing courses:

1. be explicit;
2. build in expert practices;
3. tap prior knowledge and concurrent knowledge;
4. include processes and link them to key terms and a framework;
5. consistently ask students to create their own frameworks using prior knowledge;
6. build in metacognition, verbal and visual, balancing big picture and small practices. (pp. 138-139).

There is much to like about *Writing Across Contexts: Transfer, Composition, and Sites of Writing*. Designing a writing curriculum that fosters transfer is a valuable enterprise. The curriculum developed at Florida State is thoughtful. Likewise, I appreciate the connection to Yancey's previous work on reflection and the attention to prior knowledge as a source of meaning-making. In many ways, what I liked best about this book is what came at the end, as I was less interested in the shortcomings of other first-year curricular models and more interested in how different students experienced the TFT model (i.e., what were the various affordances of the curriculum for different students?).

In considering *Writing Across Contexts: Transfer, Composition, and Sites of Writing* in relation to the future of transfer research in writing, I found myself wanting three advancements. First, I want literature that draws on other writing research traditions. The literature on transfer is vast, and it's useful to build connections to a variety of transfer and transfer-like research in the field of psychology. *How People Learn* from the National Research Council, for example, is an excellent resource. One of its co-authors, John Bransford, has spent his career working on studies of adaptive expertise. Of more interest to me, however, is that composition researchers look to literacy research in education, which has a rich research tradition on how students transfer literacy practices from home to school. Likewise, researchers working in the English for academic purposes and English for specific purposes tradition provide other ways of theorizing the development of writing knowledge, and they are especially valuable in considering the multitude of learning approaches used by culturally and linguistically diverse students. And, finally, the field of technical communication has a long tradition of investigating what practices and knowledge students transfer from college to workplace writing. All of these traditions have much to offer the transfer discussion in composition studies.

Second, I want detailed methods. While we may debate whether Haswell's (2005) argument that replicable, aggregable, and data-supported are the three features that should predominate our empirical research agenda, it can be said that the last decade might be characterized as empiricism on faith. What I mean by that is that many studies today don't have a full methods section. We learn how many students were interviewed or surveyed; we learn something about the various instruments used and we are told that the interviews or focus group data were coded by theme. What we don't hear is much about data analysis and, for studies that are trying to make generalizable claims, we rarely see any statistical analysis of survey data. Does it matter that methods go unstated? I think it does if we're moving beyond claims about localism or research for the sake of research. If we want to make large-scale curricular changes based on transfer studies, then we should be able to demonstrate a clear trajectory in our empirical projects from research question through implications. Without that connection, we're relying on curricular innovations that may not serve all students very well. In the case of *Writing Across Contexts: Transfer, Composition, and Sites of Writing*, I'd like to see an online supplement, which would be invaluable for writing program administrators looking to follow the Florida State TFT model.

Finally, in making claims about curricular change in relation to writing development, we must consider the scope of our claims. Did one course or one kind of curricular innovation really lead to changes in student writing development more generally? Under what conditions? For what kinds of students? What about the students for whom the curriculum failed? Do the gains or losses hold over time? What length of time? These are all questions that can inform transfer research, especially if we are looking for curricular solutions. What I'd like to see is a discussion of the methodological entanglements when we set out to validate certain kinds of curricular experiences—when we marry writing development research with assessment research.

In the end, Yancey et al. capture the crux of the problem with studying transfer of writing expertise: "It's not merely that situations are different; it's that situations, even when they look similar, are located in very different activity systems and are contextualized by different goals, participants, and tools" (p. 43). In our desire to make writing meaningful for students, I welcome the desire to learn what they bring to sites of writing and what they carry with them.

References

Adler-Kassner, L., Majewski, J., & Koshnick. (2012). The value of troublesome knowledge: Transfer and threshold concepts in writing and history. *Composition Forum, 26*. Retrieved from http://compositionforum.com/issue/26/troublesome-knowledge-threshold.php

Beaufort, A. (2007). *College writing and beyond: A new framework for university writing instruction.* Logan: Utah State UP.

Bergmann, L., & Zepernick, J. (2007). Disciplinarity and transfer: Students' perceptions of learning to write. *Writing Program Administration, 31*(1-2), 124-149.

Haswell, R. (2005). NCTE/CCCC's recent war on scholarship. *Written Communication. 22*(2), 198-223.

Herrington, A., & Curtis, M. (2000). *Persons in process: Four stories of writing and personal development in college.* Urbana, IL: NCTE.

Jarratt, S., Mack, K., Sartor, A., & Watson, S. (2009). Pedagogical memory: Writing, mapping, translating. *Writing Program Administration, 33*(1-2), 46-73.

Nowacek, R. (2011). *Agents of Integration: Understanding Transfer as a Rhetorical Act.* Carbondale, IL: Southern Illinois UP.

Reiff, M., & Bawarshi, A. (2011). Tracing discursive resources: How students use prior genre knowledge to negotiate new writing contexts in first-year composition. *Written Communication, 28*(3), 312-337.

Sommers, N., & Saltz, L. (2004). The novice as expert: Writing the freshman year. *College Composition and Communication, 56*(1), 124-149.

Sternglass, M. S. (1997). *Time to know them: A longitudinal study of writing and learning at the college level.* Mahwah, NJ: Erlbaum.

Walvoord, B. E., & McCarthy, L. P. (1990). *Thinking and writing in college: A naturalistic study of students in four disciplines.* Urbana, IL: NCTE.

Wardle, E. (2007). Understanding 'transfer' from FYC: Preliminary results of a longitudinal study. *Writing Program Administration, 33*(1-2), 65-85.

Contributors

Sarah N. Bryant is a mathematician by training and is currently Project Manager for an NSF ADVANCE grant "STEM-UP PA: University Partnership for the Advancement of Academic Women in Pennsylvania" and has extensive work in the area of retention and advancement issues of academic women in STEM disciplines. She has presented at the International Writing Across the Curriculum Conference and has an article with Jennifer Schaefer entitled "Becoming Successful Proof-Writers Through Peer Review, Journals, and Portfolios" that is part of a volume currently under review by the Mathematics Association of America.

Daniel Cole is Assistant Professor of Writing Studies and Composition at Hofstra University, where he has also served as WAC Director. He often teaches Writing in the Disciplines, first-year composition for engineering majors, and writing against power and oppresion. His research involves both writing pedagogy and Native American rhetoric. His work has appeared in *College Composition and Communication* and *Rhetoric Review*.

Heidi Skurat Harris is Assistant Professor of Rhetoric and Writing at the University of Arkansas at Little Rock. She specializes in online pedagogy. Prior to coming to UALR, she served as the Coordinator of Innovative Teaching Initiatives at Eastern Oregon University, where she was an associate professor. She is currently a board member of the College Composition and Communication Online Writing Instruction Effective Practices Committee, and she is an editor for the Online Open Resource for that group. She has publications in online pedagogy, critical pedagogy, and creative nonfiction.

Jacob Harris is the Media Specialist for the Pulaski Academy Library System in Little Rock, Arkansas. Prior to moving to Pulaski Academy, he was an instructor in Religious Studies at Eastern Oregon University, where he also taught in and facilitated the CORE program for at-risk students. He has taught online for eight years and specializes in using using the affective domain to reach students who might struggle with content in the classroom. He has an MLS from Indiana University and an MA in Religious Studies from Missouri State University.

Barrie E. Harvey is Visiting Assistant Professor of English at the University of Cincinnati, Blue Ash College. She teaches first-year composition courses that focus on writing about writing and discourse analysis. As part of her work with the Literacy Design Collaborative, she has recently been involved in developing materials, including writing assignments and activities, that high school instructors across disciplines can use to help make their students college-ready while still adhering to the Common Core State Standards.

Nancy Knowles is Professor of English/Writing and Director of the Oregon Writing Project at Eastern Oregon University. While principally a literary scholar focusing on early 20th century British and women's literature, she has published articles on teaching with technology in Oxford University Press's journal *Literary and Linguistic Computing* and also in the anthology *Electronic Collaboration in the Humanities* from Lawrence Erlbaum. Current research interests include dual enrollment, college-level literature instruction, and access to college success for underprepared students, and she recently presented a paper on pacifism in literature at West Point Military Academy.

Noreen Lape is Associate Provost of Academic Affairs and Director of the Writing Program at Dickinson College. As director, she has developed a Writing Associates (Fellows) Program and transformed a well-established English writing center into a multilingual writing center that offers writing tutoring in eleven languages. In addition, she administers the college's WAC/WID program and coordinates a writing-focused faculty development program. Her research interests include training tutors in emotional intelligence, using writing as a wellness practice, and designing pedagogy for a multilingual writing center. Her writing studies research has appeared in *Writing Lab Newsletter, Praxis: A Writing Center Journal*, and in the edited collection *Wellness and Writing Connections*.

Tawnya Lubbes is Assistant Professor and the English for Speakers of Other Languages Program Coordinator in the College of Education at Eastern Oregon University. She is also the director of the Center for Culturally Responsive Practices. She specializes in ESOL, Spanish, diversity, and online pedagogy. Prior to coming to EOU she taught ESOL and Spanish in Idaho for ten years. She has been actively contributing to field research on the topics of culturally responsive pedagogy, teacher identity development, and ESOL best practices and online pedagogy. Her current research centers on the stages of rural pre-service teacher identity development and how teacher identity influences the integration of culturally responsive pedagogy in K-12 classrooms.

Dan Melzer is the University Reading and Writing Coordinator at California State University Sacramento, where he coordinates the Writing Center and the WAC program and teaches composition courses. He is the author of the book *Assignments across the Curriculum* and the textbook *Exploring College Writing* and the co-author of the textbook *Everything's a Text*. His work has appeared in *College Composition and Communication, WPA: Writing Program Administration, Kairos*, and the *WAC Journal*.

Mya Poe is Assistant Professor of English at Northeastern University. Her research focuses on writing assessment, diversity, and writing in the disciplines. She is co-author of *Learning to Communicate in Science and Engineering: Case Studies From MIT*, which won the CCCC 2012 Advancement of Knowledge Award, and co-editor of *Race and Writing Assessment*, which won the 2014 CCCC Outstanding Book of the Year in the Edited Collection category. She is currently working on a book about the effects of writing assessment on diverse students and is series co-editor of the *Oxford Short Guides to Writing in the Disciplines*.

Carol Rutz directs the writing program at Carleton College in Northfield, Minnesota. Her work involves teaching writing courses for several departments and working with WAC faculty on assessment and faculty development. Recent research has involved seeking evidence that faculty development programs affect student learning as well as the teaching practices of individual faculty.

Jennifer B. Schaefer is Associate Professor of Mathematics at Dickinson College. In addition to the mathematical areas of algebraic group theory, symmetric spaces, and representation theory, her research interests include writing in the discipline. She has attended and presented at the International Writing Across the Curriculum Conference and has an article with Sarah Bryant entitled "Becoming Successful Proof-Writers Through Peer Review, Journals, and Portfolios" that is part of a volume currently under review by the Mathematics Association of America.

Laura Wilder is an associate professor of English at the University at Albany, SUNY. Her research on writing in the disciplines has appeared in *Rhetoric Review, Written Communication* and, with Joanna Wolfe, in *Research in the Teaching of English*. She and Joanna Wolfe have an introductory textbook on the rhetorical strategies of literary analysis forthcoming from Bedford/St. Martin's. Her *Rhetorical Strategies and Genre Conventions in Literary Studies: Teaching and Writing in the Disciplines* (SIUP, 2012) received the 2014 CCCC Research Impact Award.

Joanna Wolfe is Teaching Professor and Director of the Global Communication Center at Carnegie Mellon University. She is author of the textbook *Team Writing:*

A Guide to Working in Groups and (with Laura Wilder) of the forthcoming *Digging into Literature: Strategies for Analytic Reading and Writing*, both from Bedford-St. Martins.

Terry Myers Zawacki is Associate Professor Emerita of English and Director Emerita of Writing Across the Curriculum at George Mason University. Her publications include the co-authored *Engaged Writers and Dynamic Disciplines: Research on the Academic Writing Life* and the co-edited collections *WAC and Second Language Writers: Research towards Linguistically and Culturally Inclusive Programs* and *Practices and Writing Across the Curriculum: A Critical Sourcebook* as well as articles on varied WAC/WID, writing center, and writing assessment topics. She is lead editor of the International Exchanges on the Study of Writing series on the WAC Clearinghouse and also serves on the editorial board.

How to Subscribe

The WAC Journal is published annually in print by Parlor Press and Clemson University. Digital copies of the journal are simultaneously published at The WAC Clearinghouse in PDF format for free download. Print subscriptions support the ongoing publication of the journal and make it possible to offer digital copies as open access. Subscription rates: One year: $25; Three years: $65; Five years: $95. You can subscribe to *The WAC Journal* and pay securely by credit card or PayPal at the Parlor Press website: http://www.parlorpress.com/wacjournal. Or you can send your name, email address, and mailing address along with a check (payable to Parlor Press) to

> Parlor Press
> 3015 Brackenberry Drive
> Anderson SC 29621
> Email: sales@parlorpress.com

Pricing

One year: $25 | Three years: $65 | Five years: $95

Publish in The WAC Journal

The editorial board of The WAC Journal seeks WAC-related articles from across the country. Our national review board welcomes inquiries, proposals, and 3,000 to 6,000 word articles on WAC-related topics, including the following:

- WAC Techniques and Applications
- WAC Program Strategies
- WAC and WID
- WAC and Writing Centers
- Interviews and Reviews

Proposals and articles outside these categories will also be considered. Any discipline-standard documentation style (MLA, APA, etc.) is acceptable, but please follow such guidelines carefully. Submissions are managed initially via Submittable (https://parlor-press.submittable.com/submit) and then via email. For general inquiries, contact Heather Christiansen, the managing editor, via email (wacjournal@parlorpress.com). The WAC Journal is an open-access, blind, peer-viewed journal published annually by Clemson University, Parlor Press, and the WAC Clearinghouse. It is available in print through Parlor Press and online in open-access format at the WAC Clearinghouse.

PARLOR PRESS
EQUIPMENT FOR LIVING

Congratulations to These Award Winners!

GenAdmin: Theorizing WPA Identities in the Twenty-First Century
Colin Charlton, Jonikka Charlton, Tarez Samra Graban, Kathleen J. Ryan, & Amy Ferdinandt Stolley
Winner of the Best Book Award, Council of Writing Program Adminstrators (July, 2014)

Mics, Cameras, Symbolic Action: Audio-Visual Rhetoric for Writing Teachers
Bump Halbritter
Winner of the Distinguished Book Award from Computers and Composition (May, 2014)

New Releases

First-Year Composition: From Theory to Practice
Edited by Deborah Coxwell-Teague & Ronald F. Lunsford. 420 pages.
Twelve of the leading theorists in composition studies answer, in their own voices, the key question about what they hope to accomplish in a first-year composition course. Each chapter, and the accompanying syllabi, provides rich insights into the classroom practices of these theorists.

A Rhetoric for Writing Program Administrators
Edited by Rita Malenczyk. 471 pages.
Thirty-two contributors delineate the major issues and questions in the field of writing program administration and provide readers new to the field with theoretical lenses through which to view major issues and questions.

www.parlorpress.com

www.ingramcontent.com/pod-product-compliance
Lightning Source LLC
Chambersburg PA
CBHW030349170426
43202CB00010B/1304